Drawing
for All Ages

Learn to Draw Anything

Wakie Trudeau McBride

TABLELAND PRESS

Published in the USA by

TABLELAND PRESS, LLC
www.tablelandpress.com
info@tablelandpress.com

ISBN 978-1-949323-10-8 (spiral-bound)
ISBN 978-1-949323-11-5 (paperback)
ISBN 978-1-949323-12-2 (e-book)

Book Cover Design by 100 Covers

Printed in the United States of America.

*I wish to dedicate this book
to my mother, Pauline Harden Plunkett,
because she was my first artistic inspiration,
though she never knew it. She did her good deeds
without fanfare, and I so loved and appreciated
her—and she definitely did know that.*

Contents

Acknowledgements

My first acknowledgment must go to God for giving me a love for art and a love for teaching.

My second acknowledgment goes to my wonderful niece Lea Ann, without whom this book would never have been attempted. Without her encouragement and her help with a capital *H*, this book would still just be a dream. She literally taught me how to use a computer. She seemed to know how to correct any problem I could come up with, and there were plenty of those. She will never know how much help she was to me. I love her dearly and shall be eternally grateful to her.

I would like to thank my editor and publisher, Margaret Sorensen, for her patience and for all she has done to help me get my book to you.

And my dear friend Kathy, for everything.

There are many others who helped in some way: my granddaughter Joyce White, sister Vickie, my daughter Sherry and her husband Doug, my granddaughter Sarah, and my son "Doc" and his wife Mary Jo.

I want to thank all of my teachers and all of my students, even the ones eighty-five or ninety years old.

And to my beloved, precious husband, John, whom I lost while writing this book, I thank you for all the love and encouragement, just for being the man you were.

Thank you, Joe and Linda, for all of your love and prayers. And to all of my family and friends for your support and encouragement. You are the best.

Thanks to all of you who ordered the book before it was finished. Thank you for your faith in me.

INTRODUCTION

You can draw more than stick people, and you will enjoy the learning process.

How much do you want to be an artist? Are you willing to learn about shapes and form? I will be happy to show you simple drawing methods that my thirty-years-experience teaching young and old alike has taught me.

My goal is to teach you to see, really see, what is in front of you. I will help you draw it. Starting with basic shapes, you will learn to recognize those shapes and forms in things you see in life.

The instructions in this book are as important as the pictures because I will be explaining principles. If you learn the principles, you will be able to draw anything. If you try to skip this step, you can be a copier without learning the "why." The best way to learn fast is by doing the examples in sequence. You will be experiencing it as I am explaining it.

SUPPLIES

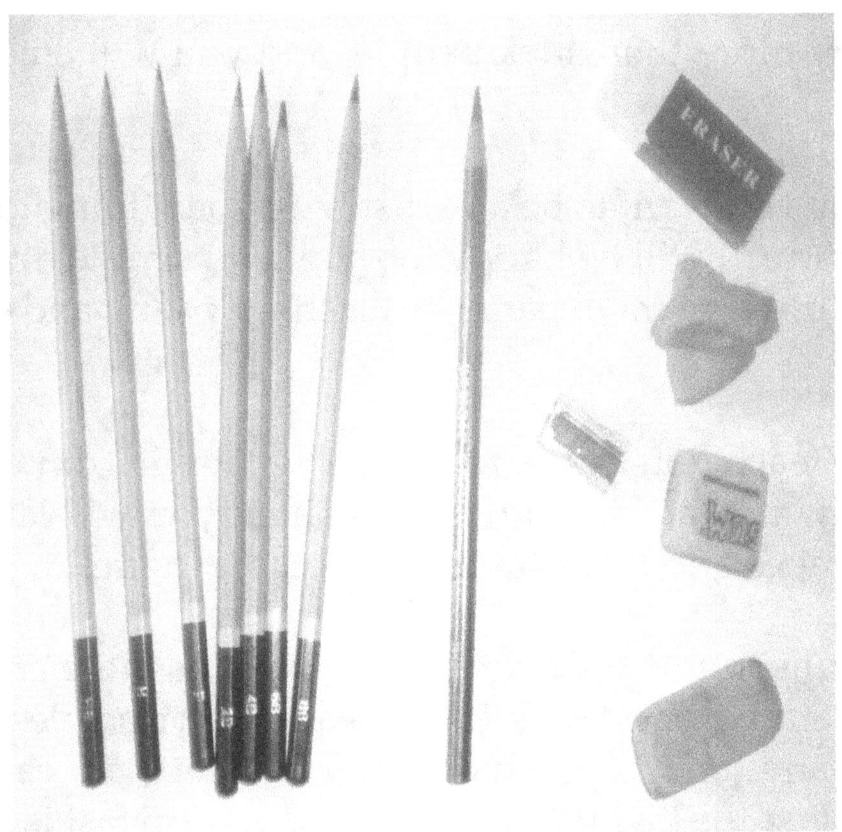

Illustration 1

These are materials we will be using: a drawing pad or paper, pencils, art erasers, pencil sharpener, and a ruler. I will explain how to use them.

Pencils used only for sketching are marked H, 2H, 3H, 4H, 5H, etc. These are hard lead and fine. The lead gets harder as the numbers get higher. When using a hard lead pencil, you will need to use a light touch. It may tear the paper if you use too much pressure.

Pencils numbered B, 2B, 3B, 4B, 5B, etc., are soft lead, and as numbers get higher, the lead gets bigger and softer. These are used for shading. The ebony pencil is soft and black and is best for dark shading.

A pencil marked F has a fine point, while a pencil marked HB is comparable to a #2 pencil. A #2 pencil (or #4H or #6H) will be a good one to use for sketching.

Art erasers are available at your local art dealer. See the right side of Illustration 1. The white eraser with a black band around it is good for everything. Second from top is a kneaded eraser (it can be cleaned by kneading it). You fold it over, squeeze it, and pull it. Repeat until clean. It is good for light erasing. The art gum eraser is good for any kind of erasing, but it crumbles. The pink one is a good all-around eraser but hard. Pick one or two you think you will like, and try them. Always use an art eraser for all art.

Between the pencils and erasers is a small manual pencil sharpener. I prefer using an electric sharpener. It produces a longer, sharper point.

CIRCLES

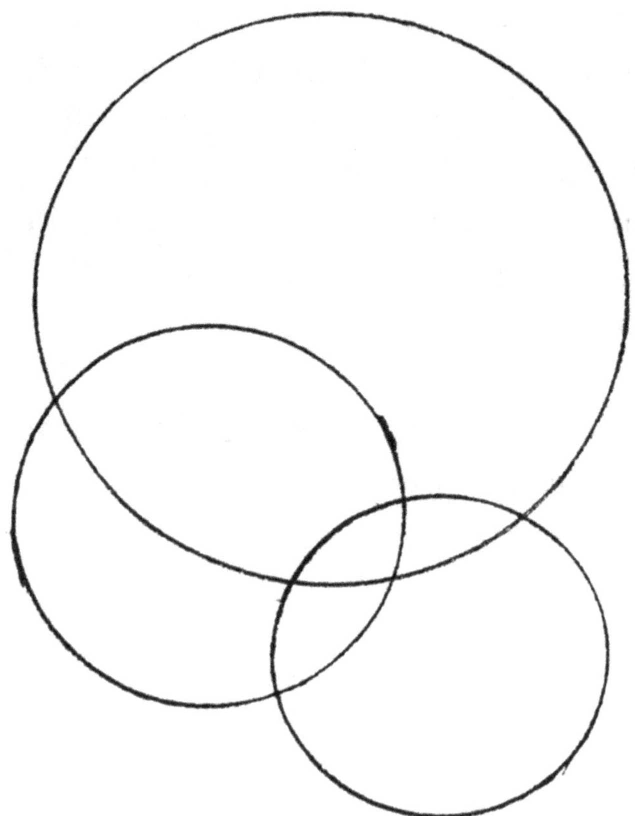

Illustration 2

You can learn how to draw a circle freehand, that is, without special tools. You could use a special tool, but this is a drawing book, so let's try it.

There is no incorrect way to hold your pencil. Take a pencil in your hand the way it is easy and comfortable. If you are young and mirror right sometimes, you might just try this one with the book turned upside down. Do this only if you are having trouble.

Look closely at Illustrations 3–5 and follow instructions that are given with each one.

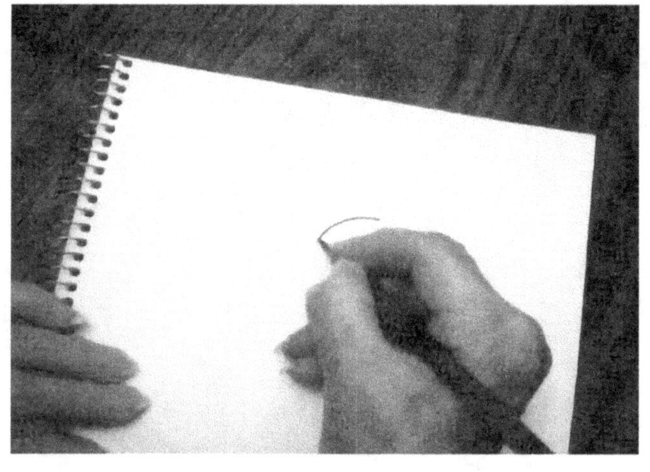

Illustration 3

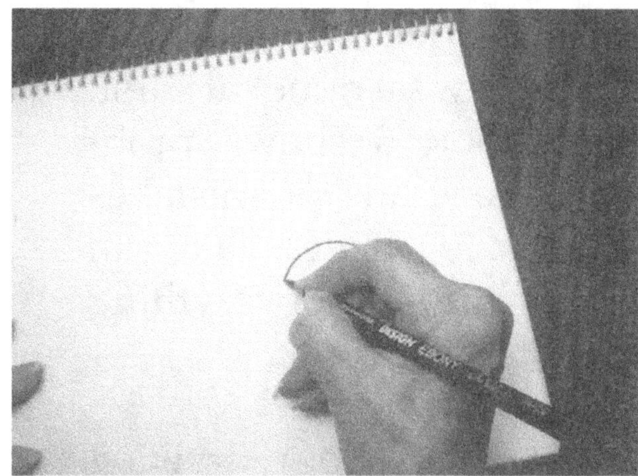

Illustration 4

Illustration 3: Draw a slightly curved (1–1½ inch) line without changing the position of your hand. Move only the wrist.

Illustration 4: Turn the paper with the other hand. Back up ¼ inch on the curved line you have already drawn. Extend the curved line another inch, keeping your drawing hand in the same position.

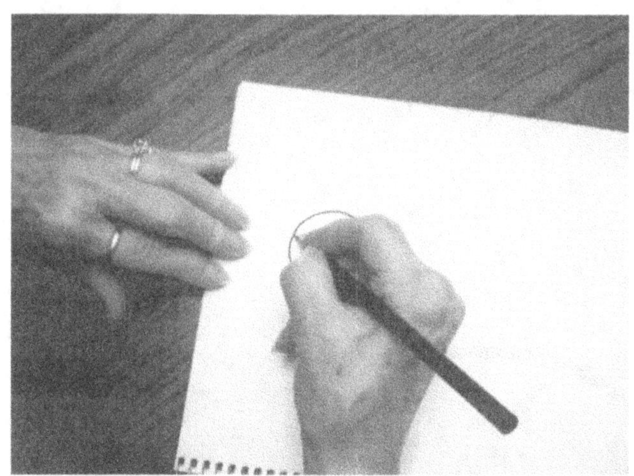

Illustration 5: Keep turning the paper until the circle is complete. Only move your wrist to extend the curved line.

Illustration 5

This will be a new process, so follow closely. Once you have done it, you can draw a circle anytime and anywhere. The trick is when you feel your thumb and forefinger putting pressure on the pencil, stop! Turn the paper farther to the right, and start drawing again. Extend the curved line another inch. Keep doing this until you meet the starting point. You have drawn a circle freehand. That is impressive.

It isn't perfectly round, is it? Neither was mine at first. Illustration 6 shows probably the kinds of mistakes you have made. Take an eraser and erase everything except the circle.

Try it again. Your drawing will improve with practice. You can make large or small circles depending on the size of your first stroke.

The circle you have drawn is a two-dimensional circle on a two-dimensional piece of paper. It has height and width. I want to introduce you to three dimensions.

Use the circle you have already drawn, or you can draw a new one.

Shade the circle by placing the point of your pencil at the inside edge of the circle. The outside edge will naturally be the darkest part of the circle, as it should be. As you continue shading the circle, it will look more like a ball.

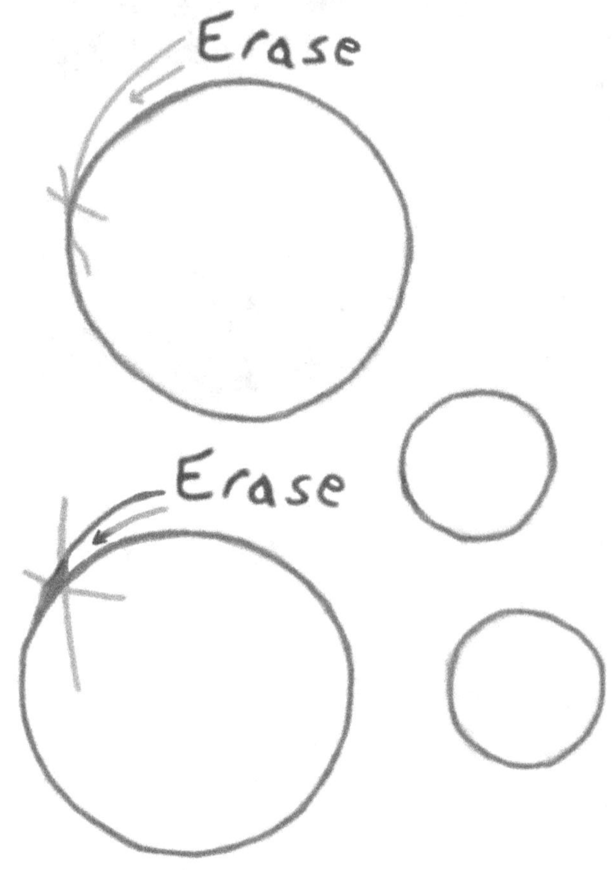

Illustration 6

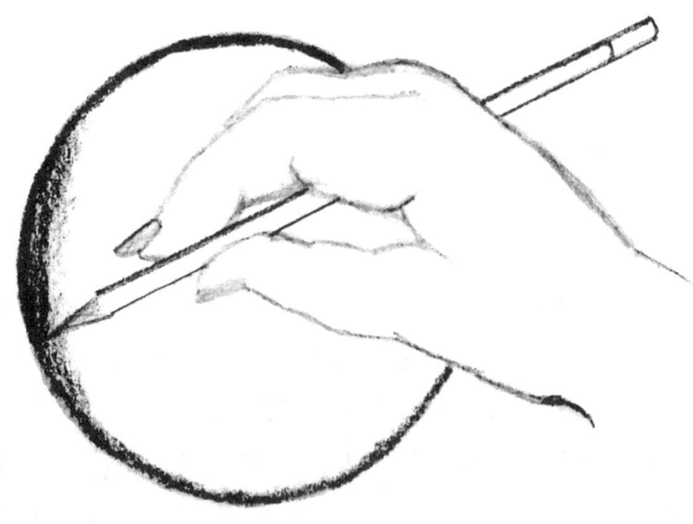

Illustration 7

Let's say the light source is to the upper left. You will need to shade darker on the bottom right and shade lighter as you go up and left. Leave a white spot for a highlight in the upper left quarter.

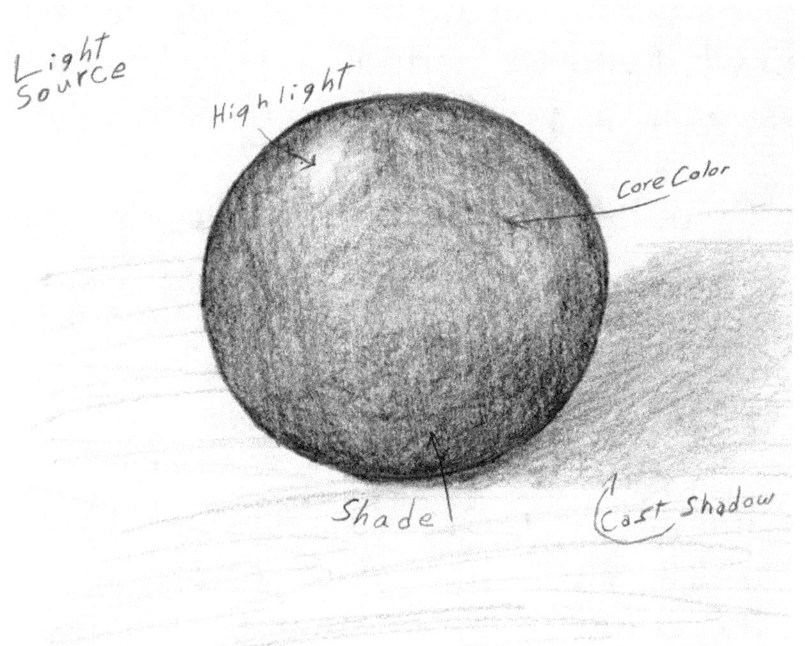

In Illustration 8, note that we have a highlight, core (the color of the ball), shade, and a cast shadow. The ball has cast a shadow opposite from the light source.

Illustration 8

This is an exercise that will help your perspective. Place a ball on a table in front of you with one light source. Have only one window or all windows covered but one. Turn off all lights. Squint your eyes and look at the ball. You will see that most shading is on one side of the ball. Can you see that? When you are squinting, you will notice that the ball has a darker line at the bottom where the ball and table meet. This is an exaggeration. But I want you to see what happens when you have only one light source.

Using shading when drawing a ball will make the circle no longer appear to have just two dimensions. Not only does it have height and width, but it appears to have depth also. It appears to have three dimensions. Casting a shadow indicates the ball is resting on a solid surface. Add horizontal lines to indicate that surface. You have made a shape (a circle that takes the form of a ball).

DAISIES FROM CIRCLES

You have drawn a circle and shaded it. You are on your way. Start to draw all kinds of things from what you are learning. Begin sketching daisies by drawing a circle as a starting point, but don't shade it.

Illustration 9

It will be easy to draw any flower similar to a daisy. Draw a circle only if the flower is facing you. If the flower is turned away from you, the center will not be a circle.

Illustration 9: Draw a circle in a circle, which will be the center of the flower and guide for the length of the petals.

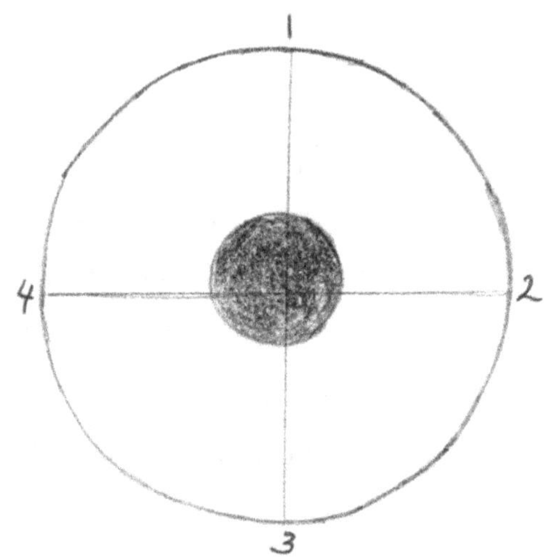

Illustration 10

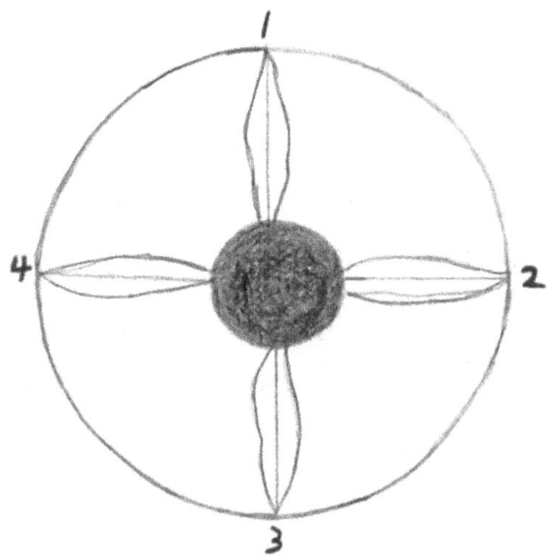

Illustration 11

Draw a vertical and horizontal line across the center of the circle, making four lines coming out from the center.

Draw a petal on each of the four lines. The large circle is used as a guide for the length of the petals. They are #1, 2, 3, and 4.

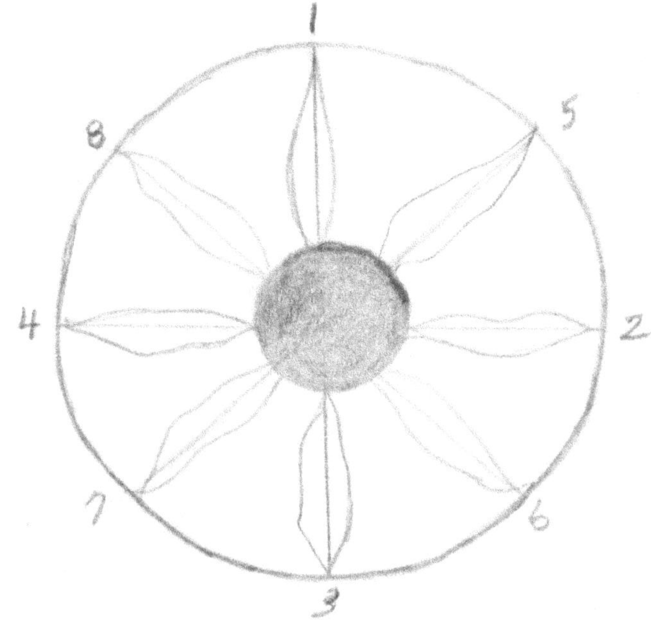

Illustration 12

Place a petal halfway between each of the numbered ones. You now have eight petals.

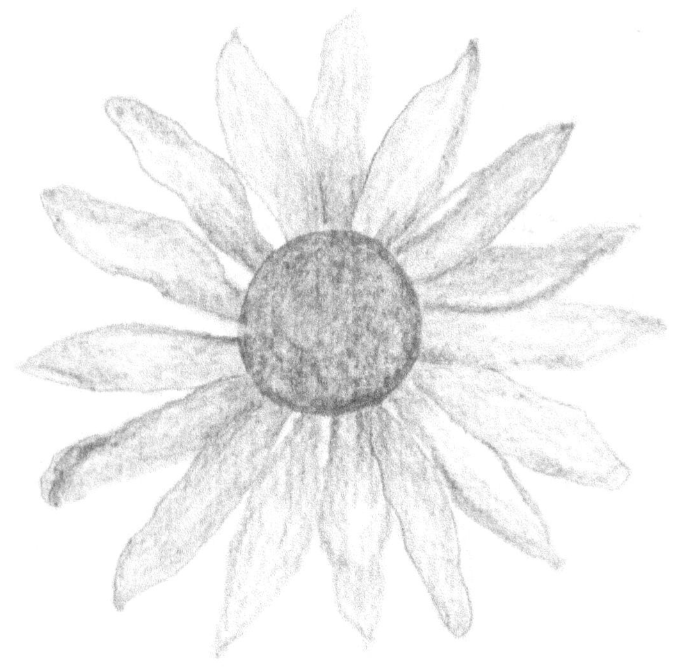

Illustration 13

Put one petal, and only one, between each numbered petal to make sixteen petals.

You have finished drawing a daisy. You may color in the petals or leave them white, as are most daises.

OVALS

I want to introduce you to the oval. If you flatten a circle a bit, it becomes an oval. Draw a page or two of ovals.

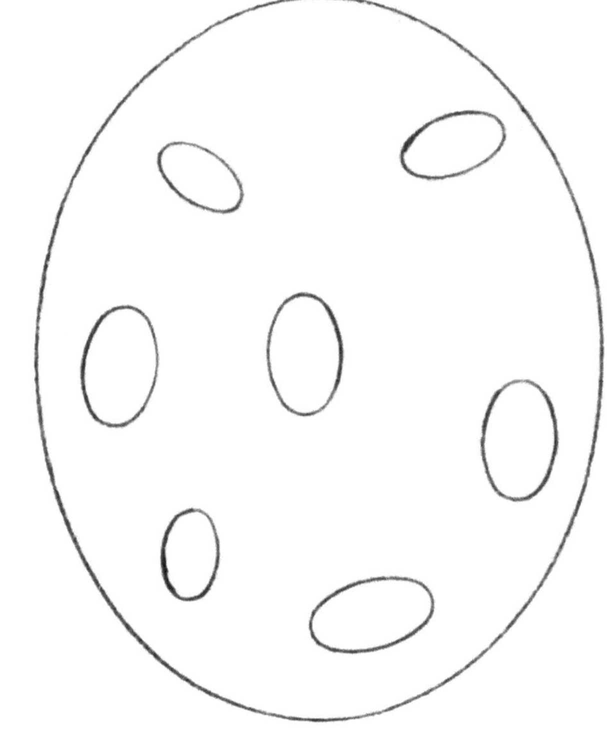

Illustration 14

You will see an oval more in nature and art than you will the circle. That is because the circle, square, or triangle automatically draws the eye to them. If, in your drawing, any of those shapes is not your intended focal point, then be careful about putting one of them in your composition.

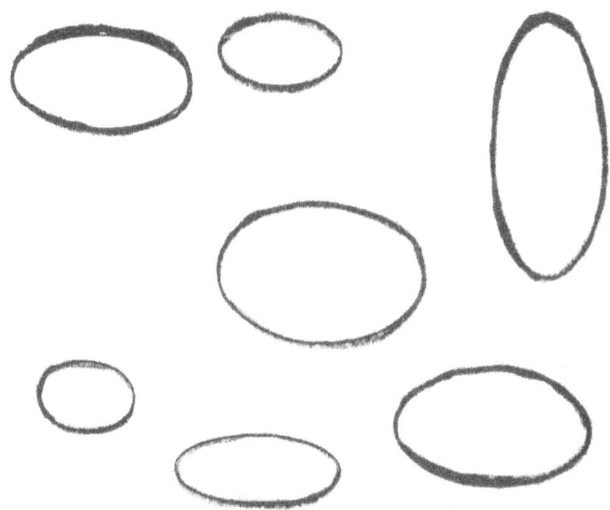

Illustration 15

LEMONS FROM OVALS

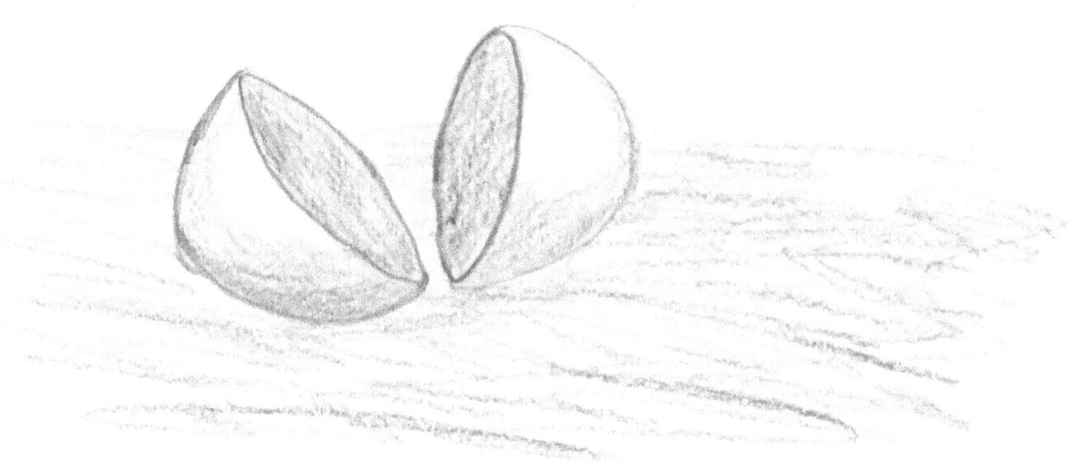

Illustration 16

The next step will be to draw a lemon. We will start by drawing an oval. To draw half a lemon, shape the cut half into another oval.

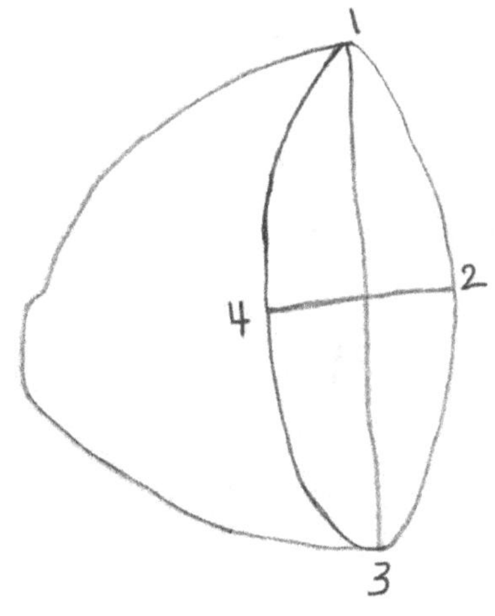

Illustration 17

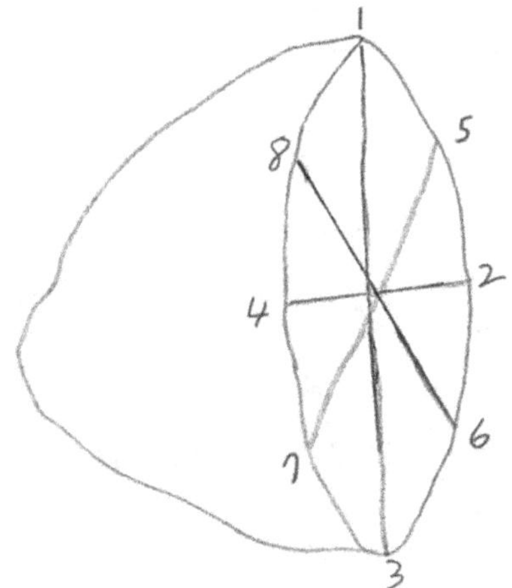

Illustration 18

Draw a vertical and horizontal line across the cut part of the lemon, and number the points 1, 2, 3, and 4.

Draw an *X* between the horizontal and vertical lines. There are eight sections shown.

Illustration 19 is an enlarged section partly filled with small teardrops. It shows what the sections look like up close. Fill all the sections with teardrops. You could add drops of juice to make it natural. Add a bigger teardrop or two.

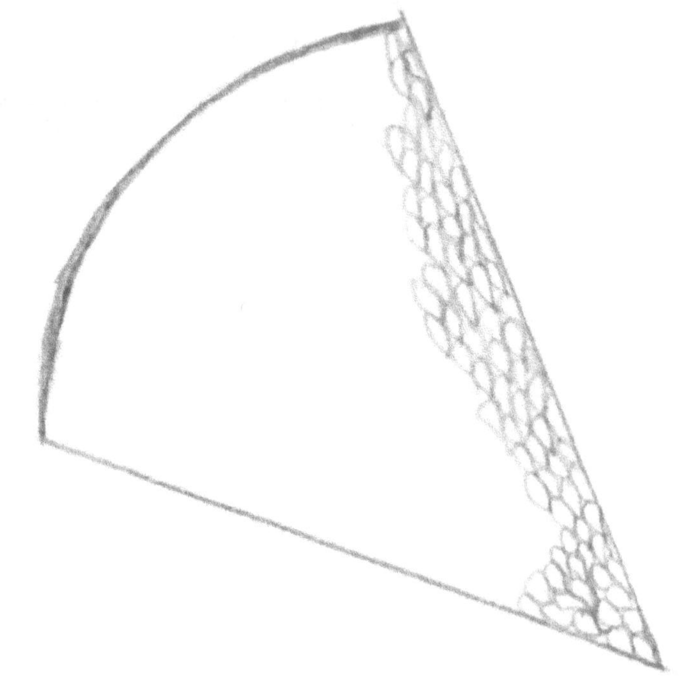

Illustration 19

We have half a lemon with all sections drawn. Shade it and set it down. You are doing great!

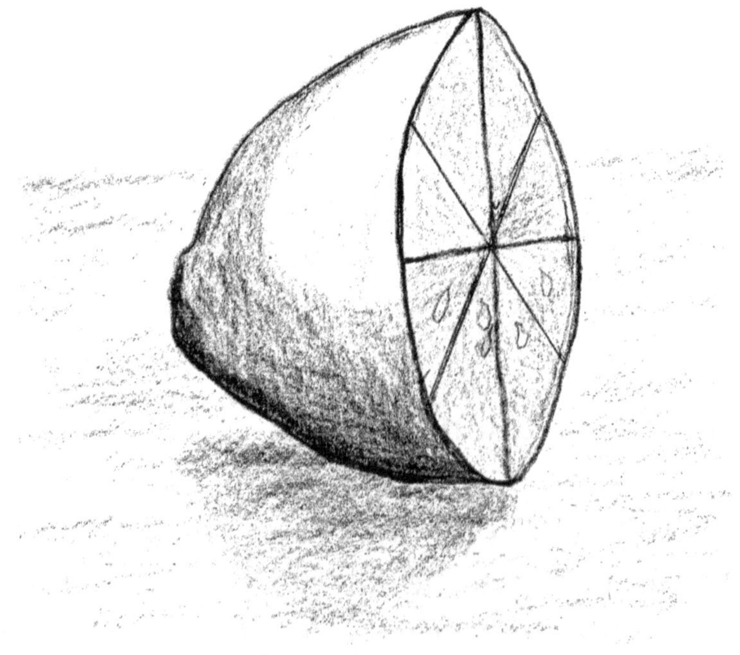

Illustration 20

TOADSTOOLS

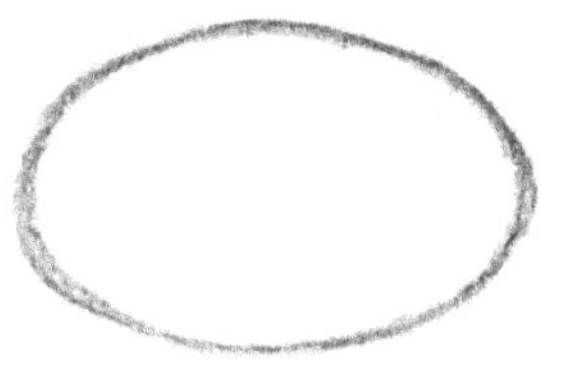

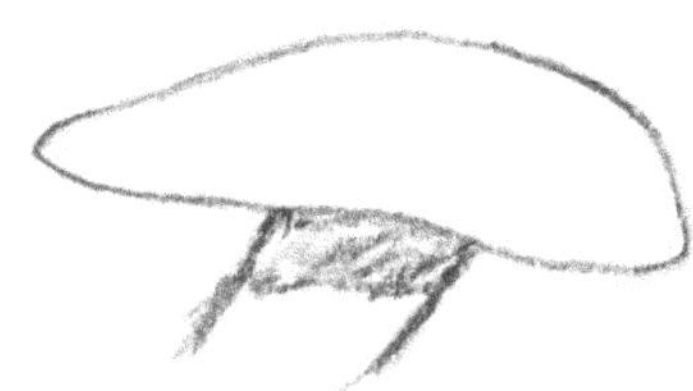

The next object is simple. You will need very little help with this. Draw an oval. Round off the edges, and with variation, you have drawn a toadstool or mushroom.

Illustration 21

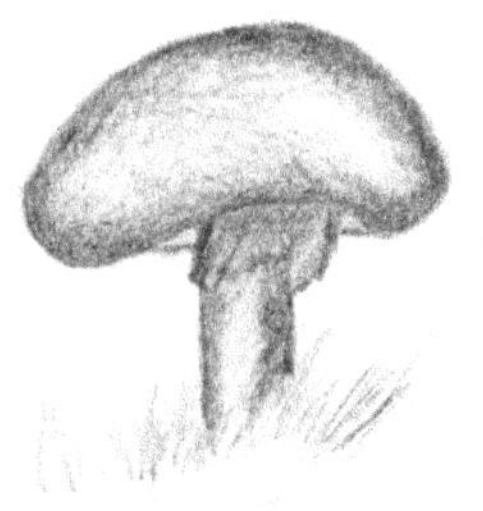

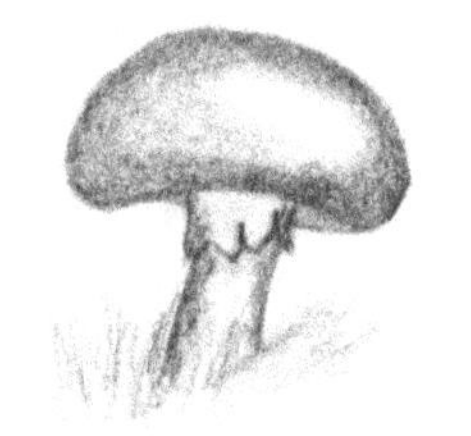

Shade it, shape it, and put grass under it. There are different species, all shaped differently.

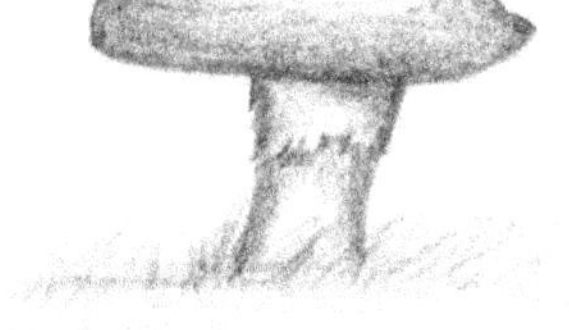

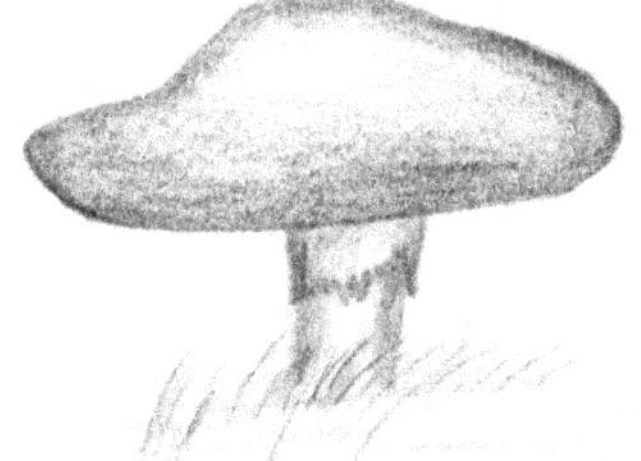

Illustration 22

GLASSES FROM OVALS

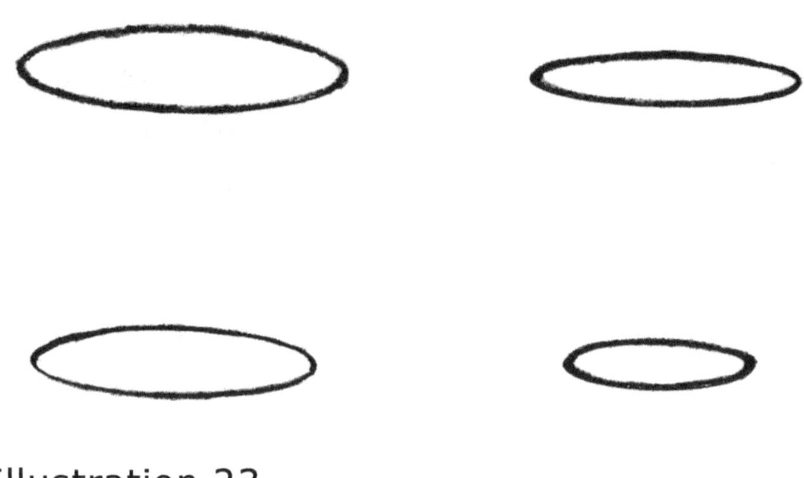

Illustration 23

Would you like to draw a glass? Draw one oval and another smaller one about four inches below that.

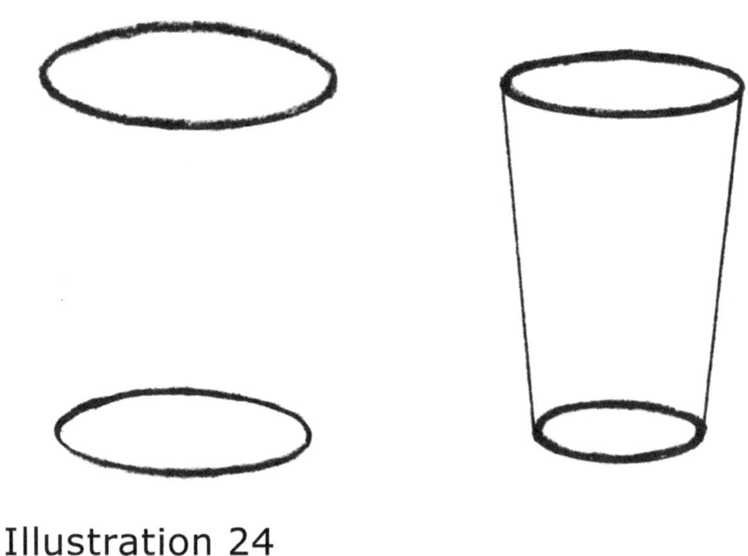

Illustration 24

Illustration 24: Connect the two ovals by drawing a line on both sides.

Illustration 25: Shade the glass inside the left side. Shade it heavier on the right, and shade the top inside in the center part. Cast a shadow,

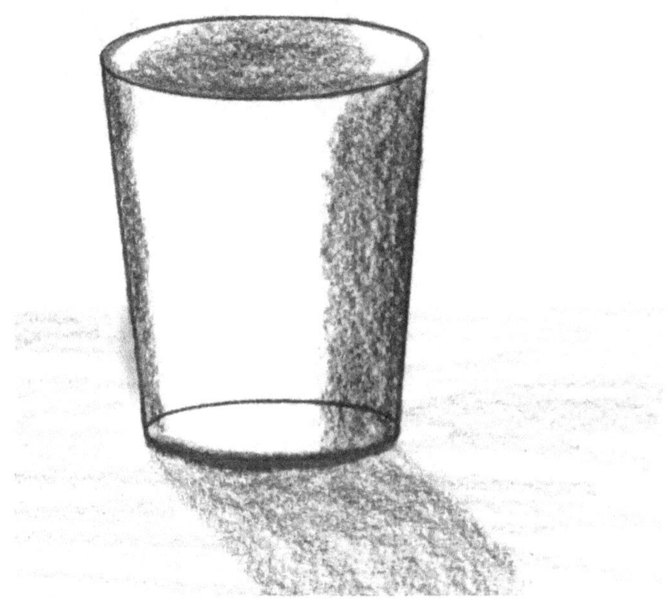

Illustration 25

and make horizontal lines to indicate a table. Make the bottom of the glass darker to show it is sitting on a solid surface.

Wasn't that easy? You have just drawn a glass. It becomes easier as you learn about shapes and how you create something else from those shapes.

Observe the glass, and you will see the bottom of the glass cannot be drawn with a straight line, even though we know it is flat. It needs to be drawn with an oval to make it appear to have depth. My job is to teach you to see that.

An interesting thing to do is set a glass in a window. Draw it just as you see it. It will be more interesting if you fill the glass about two-thirds full of water. It is fascinating how many reflections you can see. Draw all the reflections in the glass. Did you ever notice them before?

To make it more challenging, place a spoon in the glass. Do you see what happened to the spoon? The handle looks like it is broken. I'll explain it this way. The light reflects differently through water and glass than it does just through the glass.

15

You can expand the glass and make a goblet easily.

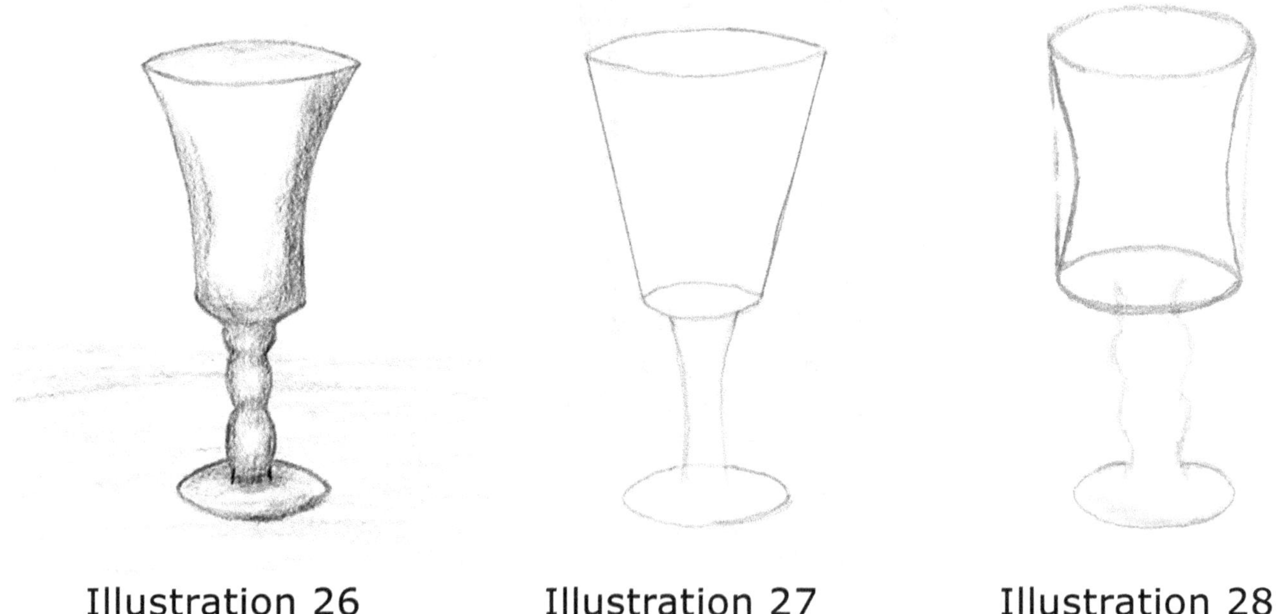

Illustration 26   Illustration 27   Illustration 28

Can you see how it was done? We have added a stem and shaped
the goblet.

Look at a variety of goblets. Some have different tops, and others
have variously shaped stems. Start by making the glass, and bring
the sides in (curved or straight). Draw the bottom oval smaller. I have
slanted the sides of the goblet. Make the sides curve in more. You may
draw either or both.

Use the same shading as you did
on the tumbler. Shade it, and it
is finished. Very good!

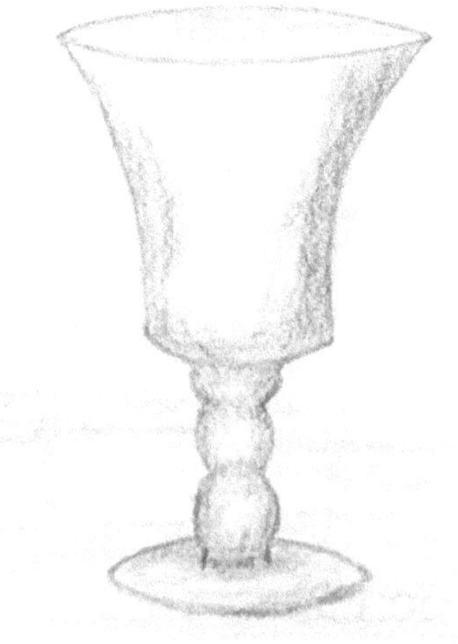

Illustration 29

FLOWERS FROM CIRCLES AND OVALS

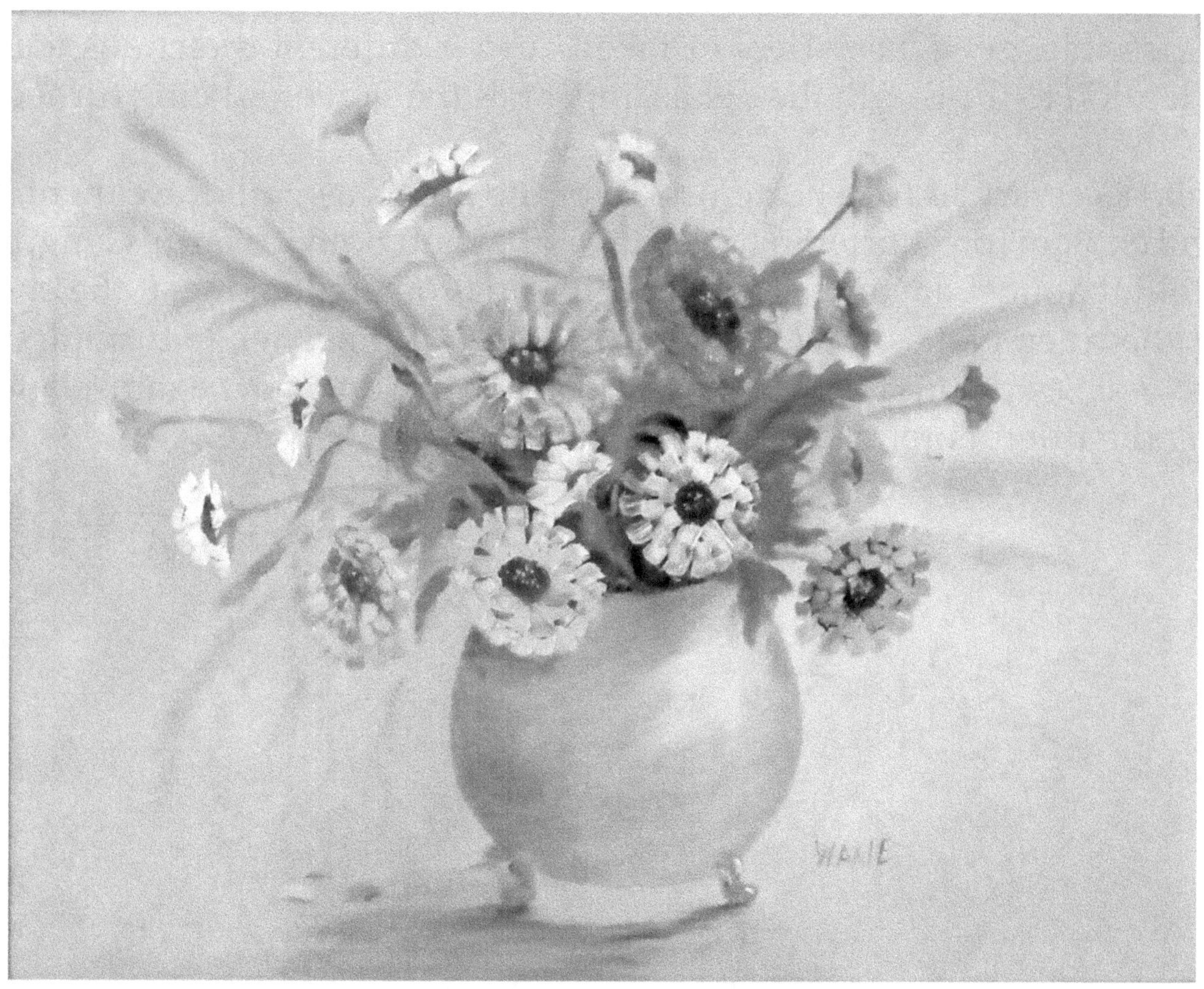

Illustration 30: *Mom's Bouquet,* oil. These are zenias.

Look at floral paintings done with circles and ovals. These are flowers with round centers, which are turned in various directions. Notice some look like circles and some like ovals. Draw each flower to appear to turn in a different direction. You do this by drawing the center and the outside oval the same proportions. The outside circle or oval is a guide for the length of the petals. Use the same principle that you used for drawing the daisy. We just take it a step farther. We are turning them in all directions.

Daisy

If possible, get a daisy (real or fake). Turn it different directions. Pay attention to the length the petals appear as the flower is being turned.

It is necessary to foreshorten some of the petals as you draw them. I will explain foreshortening. Pick up a ruler and hold it at arm's length. Hold it almost flat and slowly turn it until you are looking at the end of the ruler. Notice how long it appears at all times while turning it. Do you see the difference? If not, close one eye and do it again, slanting the ruler more.

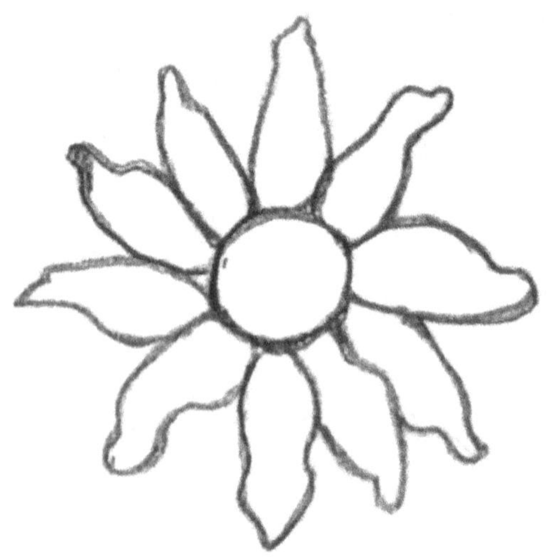

Illustration 31

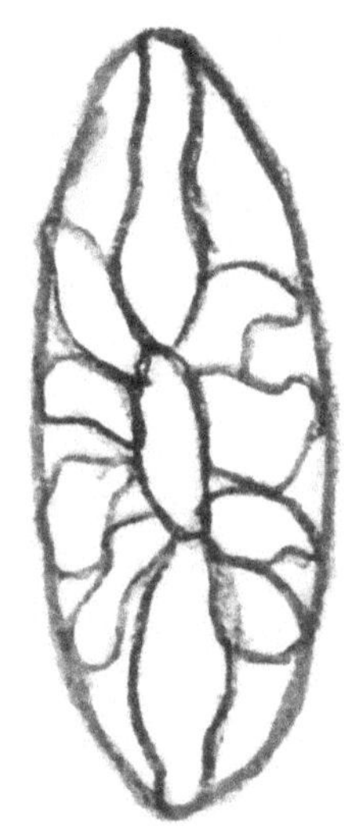

Illustration 32

It has to do with perspective, and we will cover that a little later. Make one oval inside another. Use the larger oval as a guide for the length of the petals. Erase the outside oval when you are finished drawing the flower.

Vary the shape of the petals. Don't make them all the same. This is called repetition with variation. It will make the drawing more interesting. Use your creativity to change two or three petals. Make some

curl up on the edge or at the end. See illustrations 31 and 32 to see
how to make them shaped differently. Generally speaking, anytime
you can make a variance in a series of things that are alike, without
hurting the overall appearance, you will improve the composition.

As you look at the following painting, I will explain things that will
be helpful as you learn more about art.

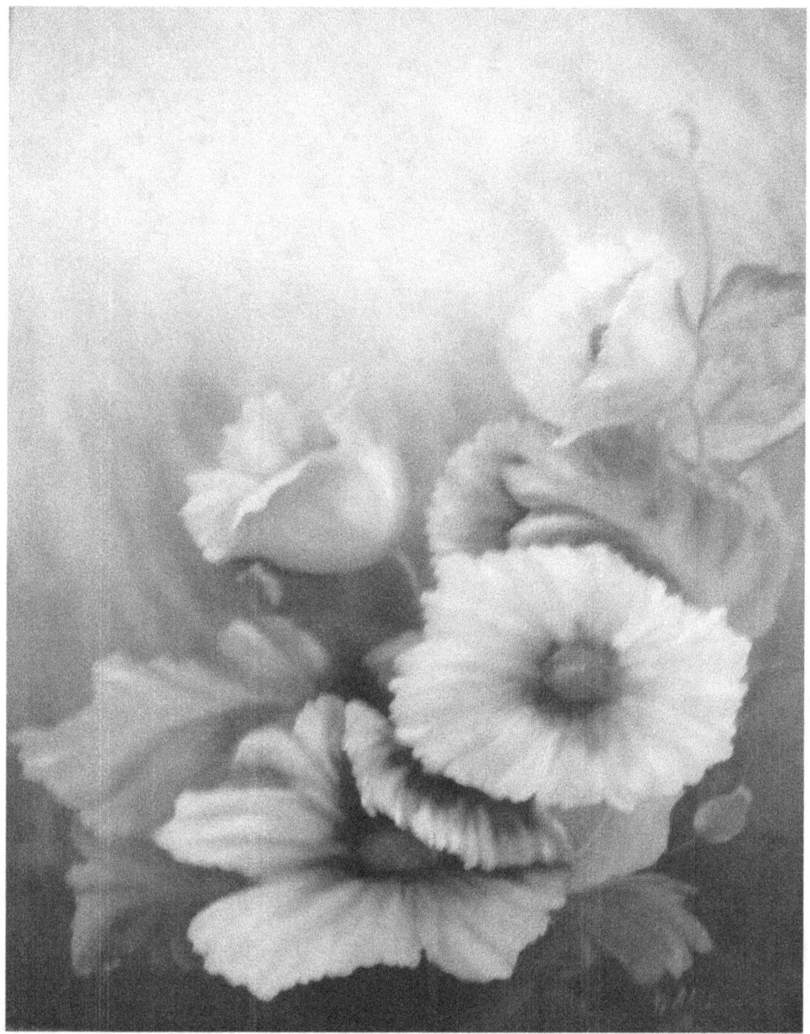

Illustration 33: *Passion*, oil

Can you see two blossoms in the forefront of the painting? These are
called foreground. The rest of the flowers are in the middle ground.
The blurred part of the picture is background. Notice one of the petals
of the bottom flower is turned under and another one is barely visible. This is one way to vary the flowers in a composition.

Jonquil

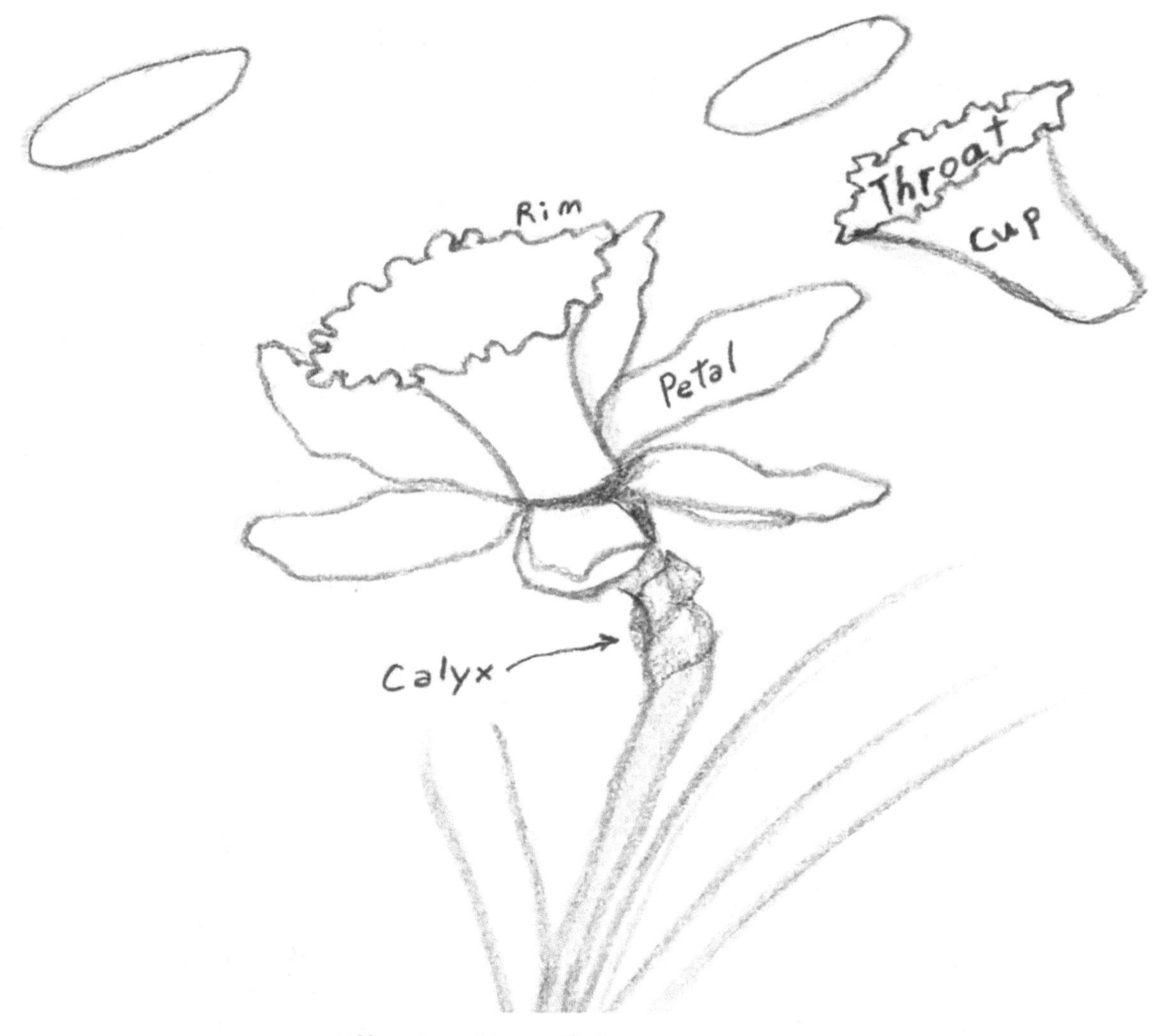

Illustration 34

Illustration 34 is a jonquil with the cup, the throat of the cup, the rim of the cup, the petal, and the calyx named for you.

Notice where the petal starts out from the cup and how it is shaped. Draw the six petals. The calyx is the onion-like skin below the bloom that covers the bud until the bud opens to reveal the blossom. It stays on the stem. When shading the calyx, shade it lightly. It is almost transparent.

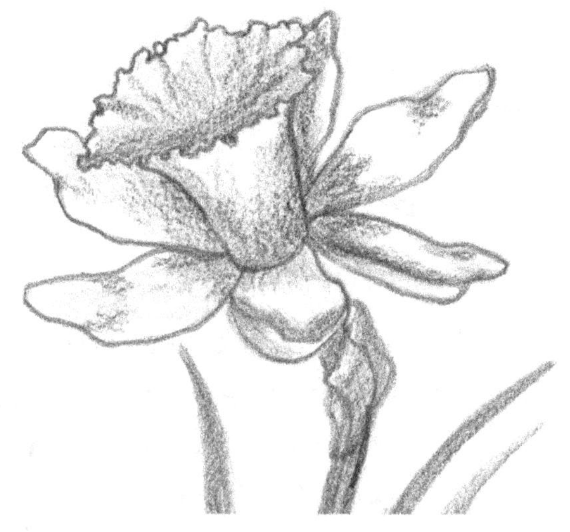

Shading is important. Shade inside the cup of the blossom, getting lighter as you reach the top. Notice how it has darker shading near the top in lines and how these lines come at special places. They begin at the dips in the ruffled edge and go toward the bottom of the cup.

Illustration 35

You will need to shade the bottom of the cup and down each side. Shade the petals where they come out from the bottom of the cup. Also, shade any petal or part of a petal that starts behind something.

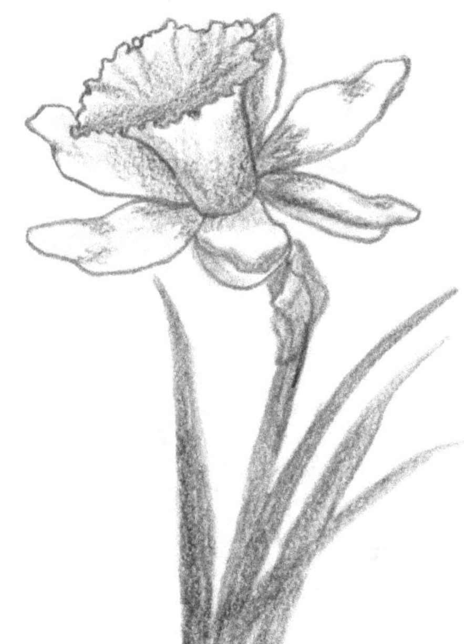
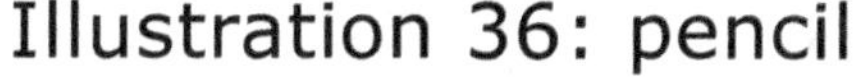

Illustration 36: pencil

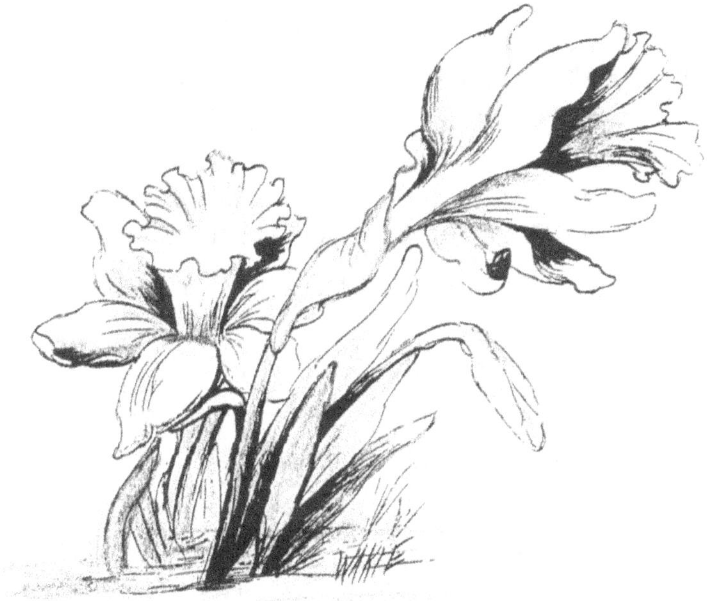

Illustration 37: *Playful Jonquil*, ink

Draw the stem and the blades. Shade all of it. You have just finished drawing and shading a jonquil.

Illustration 37 is a more playful drawing, but still a jonquil.

TEARDROPS

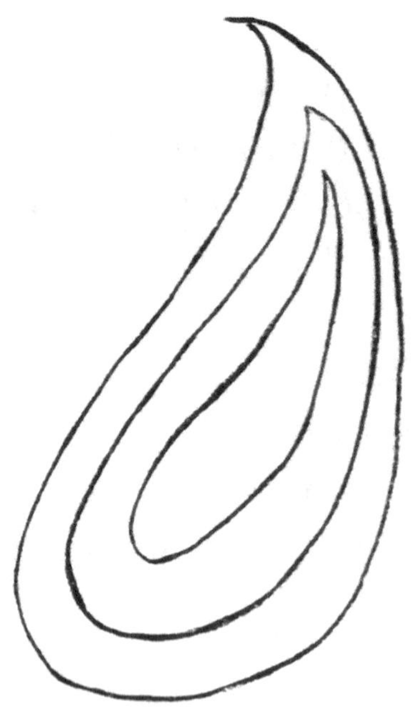

Illustration 38

The teardrop is as if you had pinched up one end of an oval. Look at the teardrop. I want you to look at it, think about it, and memorize it. Now I want you to close your eyes. Can you still see it? That is called visualizing.

Many things begin with a teardrop. I want you to learn to draw it until you are comfortable with it. Draw it lying on one side, then the other side, and upside down. Start drawing at the part that goes in first. Just loop it around. Now, let's have fun with teardrops.

Draw a page or two of them. Do you see how easy it can be?

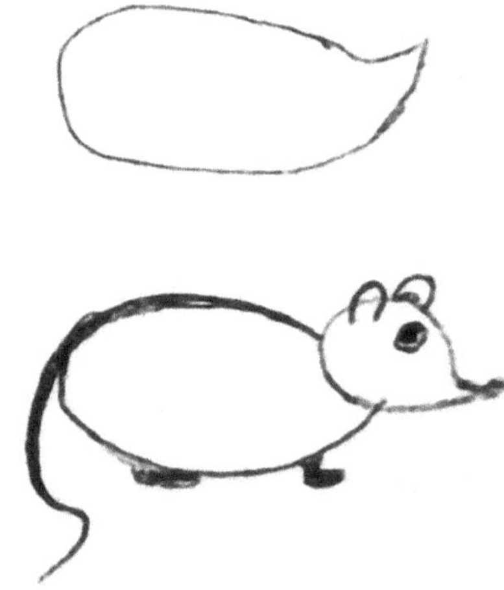

Illustration 39

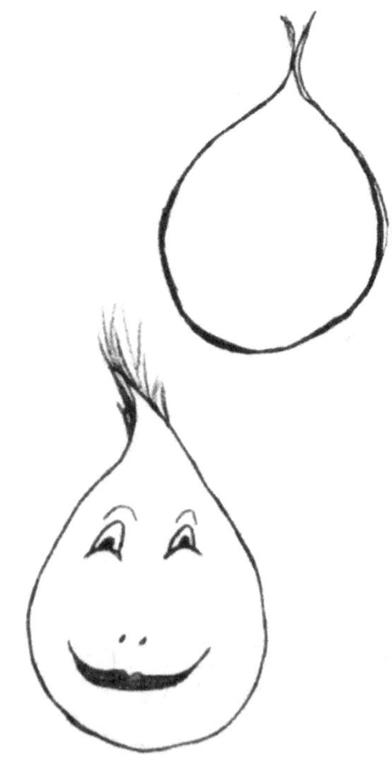

Illustration 40

FISH FROM TEARDROPS

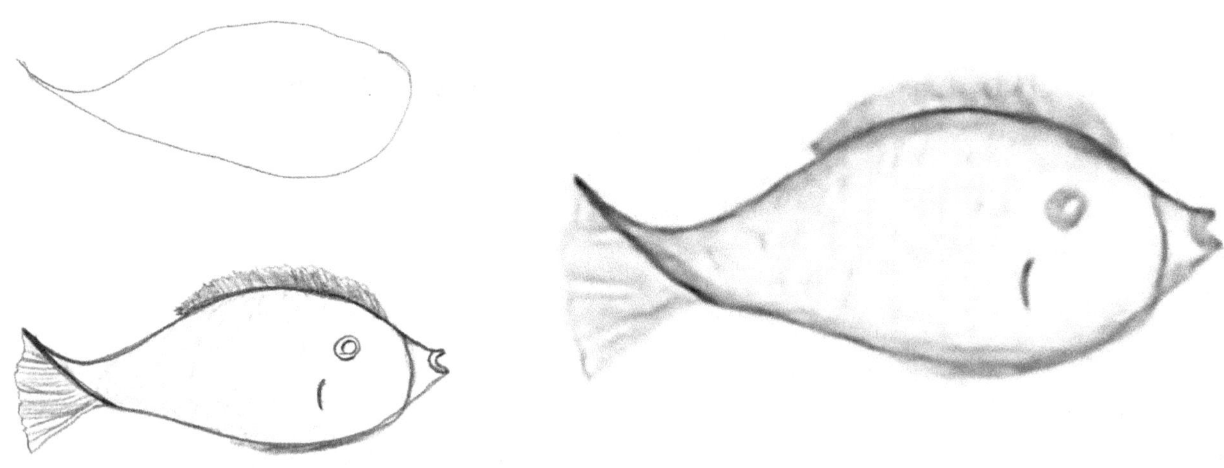

Illustration 41   Illustration 42

Draw a teardrop. Add an eye, a mouth, fins, gills, and a tail. Shade it, and it is finished.

Draw another kind of fish.

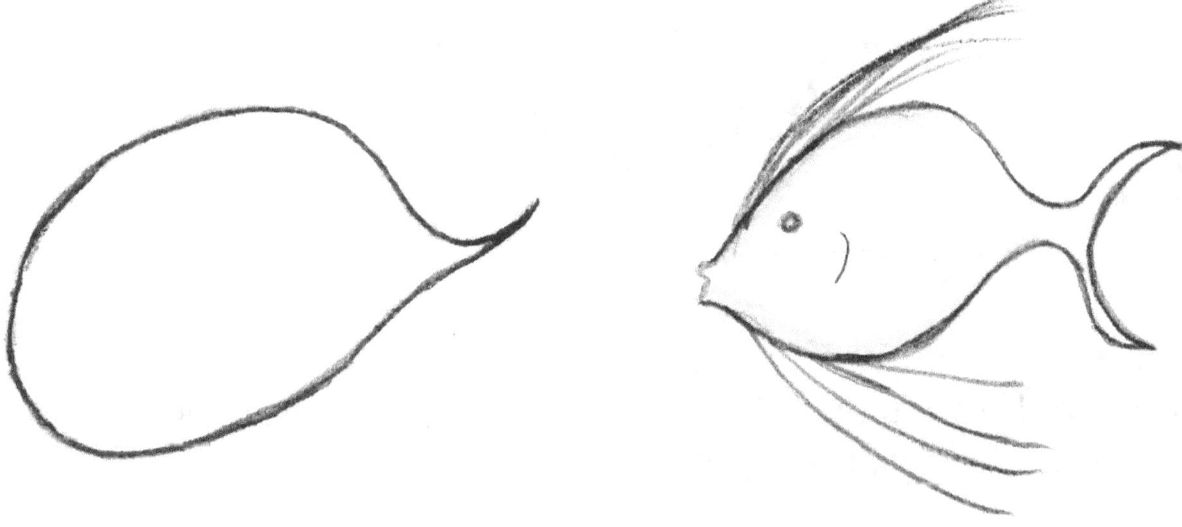

Illustration 43   Illustration 44

BIRDS FROM TEARDROPS

Almost every species of birds will fit into the teardrop category. See how completely a bird can be drawn with just three teardrops? You will have to vary the teardrop shape for some birds.

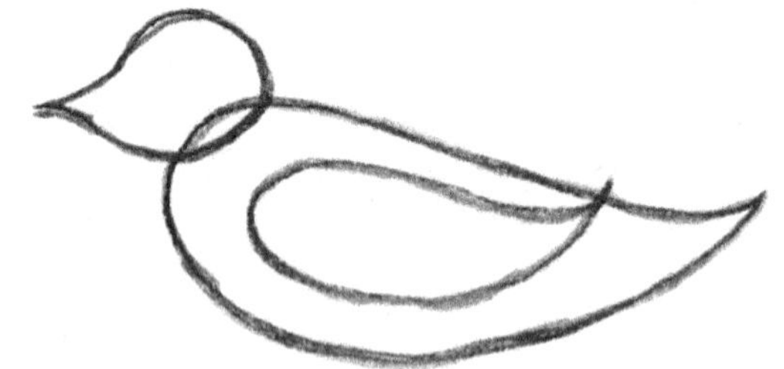

Illustration 45

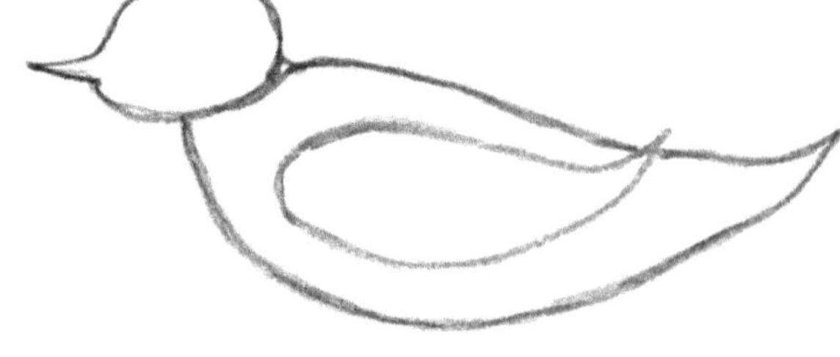

Illustration 46

Illustration 46: Erase the overlap of the head and the body.

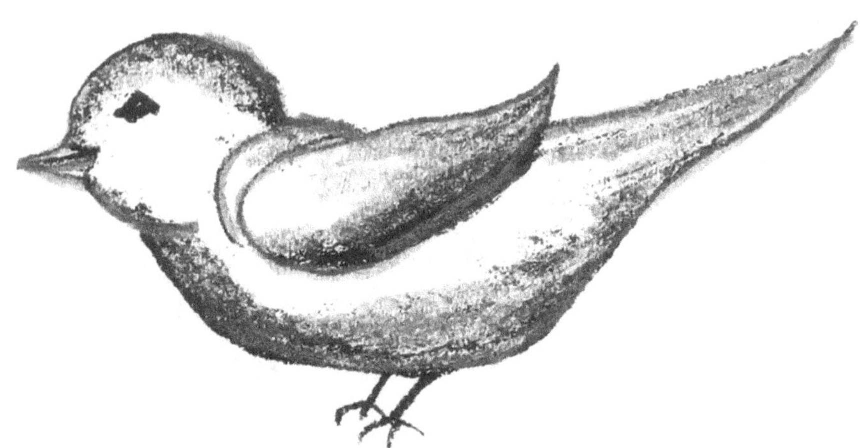

Illustration 47

Put in the eye and beak. Shade it and put legs on it. Put the legs far enough back to balance the bird but not far enough for him to fall backward. You have just drawn a bird!

Draw some other kinds of birds. They all start with three teardrops.

The Wren is a small bird. Most of
the time, its tail is sticking up, and
it is singing. Draw its eye, beak,
legs, and feet.

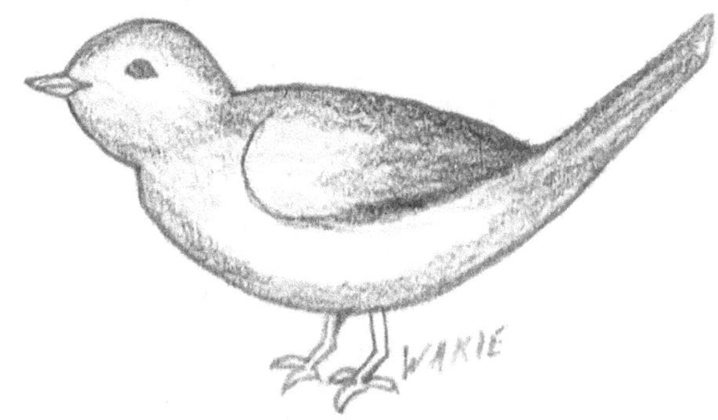

Illustration 48

The red Cardinal can be drawn
the same, though it is thicker
through the middle. This is the
type of things you will need to
notice in your investigation. Put a
topknot on its head and the black
part behind its beak, and shade it.

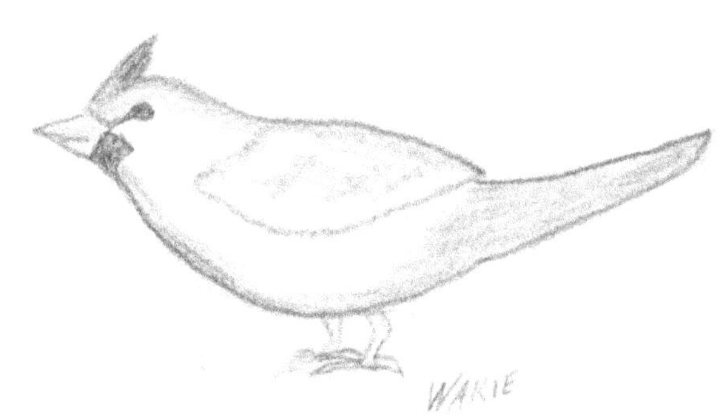

Illustration 49

The Scissor-tailed Flycatcher can
be started the same way, only its
tail extends longer. It can still be
started with teardrops. Shade it,
and you are finished.

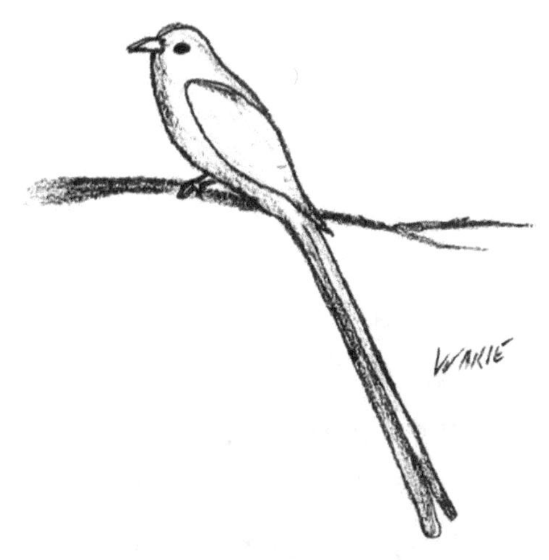

Illustration 50

Anything (birds, balls, horses, and animals) that visually ends with
a line but evidently continues on around to the other side has to be
shaded on the inside of the outside line. Put the point of the pencil on
the inside edge of that line. Start shading at this point.

25

Swan

The swan has graceful lines and can be started with two teardrops.

Look closely at the next few drawings. See if you can get the position right on the placement of the two teardrops for the head and the body.

Put it together one step at a time. Draw the bottom lightly because that part will be underwater. Draw another small teardrop for his head.

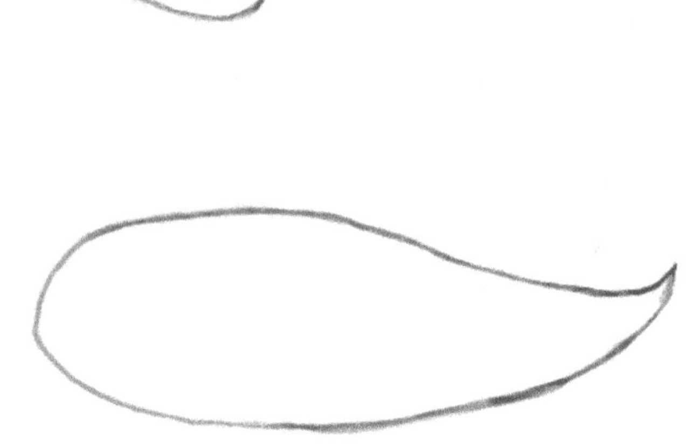

Illustration 51

Draw the neck by drawing two lines down from the head. The first line starts at the center of the head and curves first to the right and then left and comes into the bottom of the chest. The other one starts at the back of the head, and you can see where it joins his back.

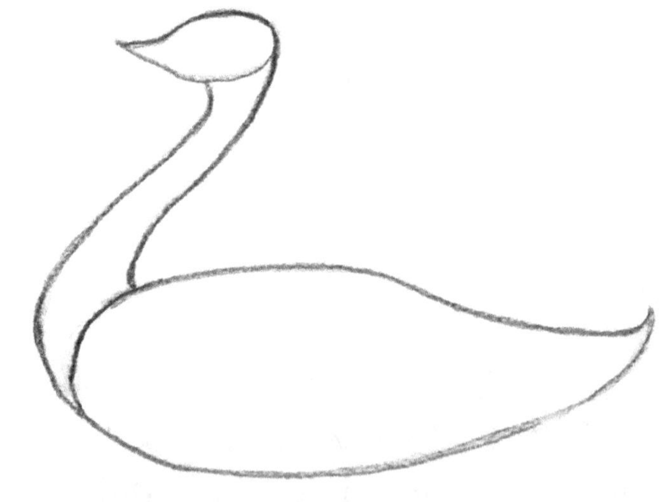

Illustration 52

Pay close attention to the hump on top of the beak. Draw the hump up to, and including, the eye. Finish the wing. It is also a teardrop shape. Did you notice? Put some horizontal lines to indicate the water.

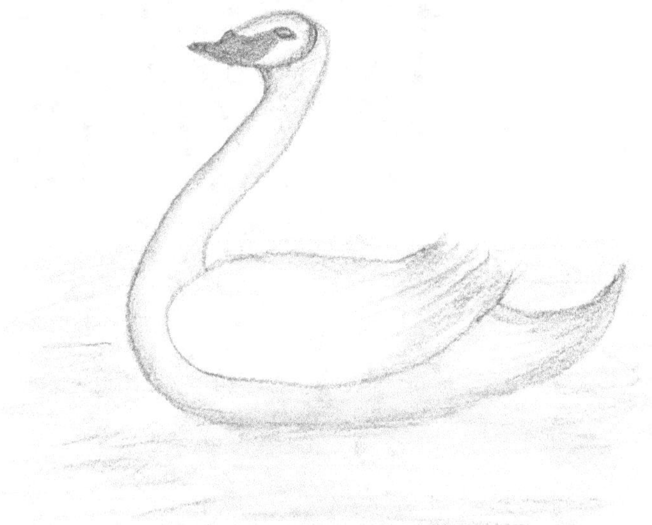

Illustration 53

Here are some paintings of swans done in different mediums and in different ways.

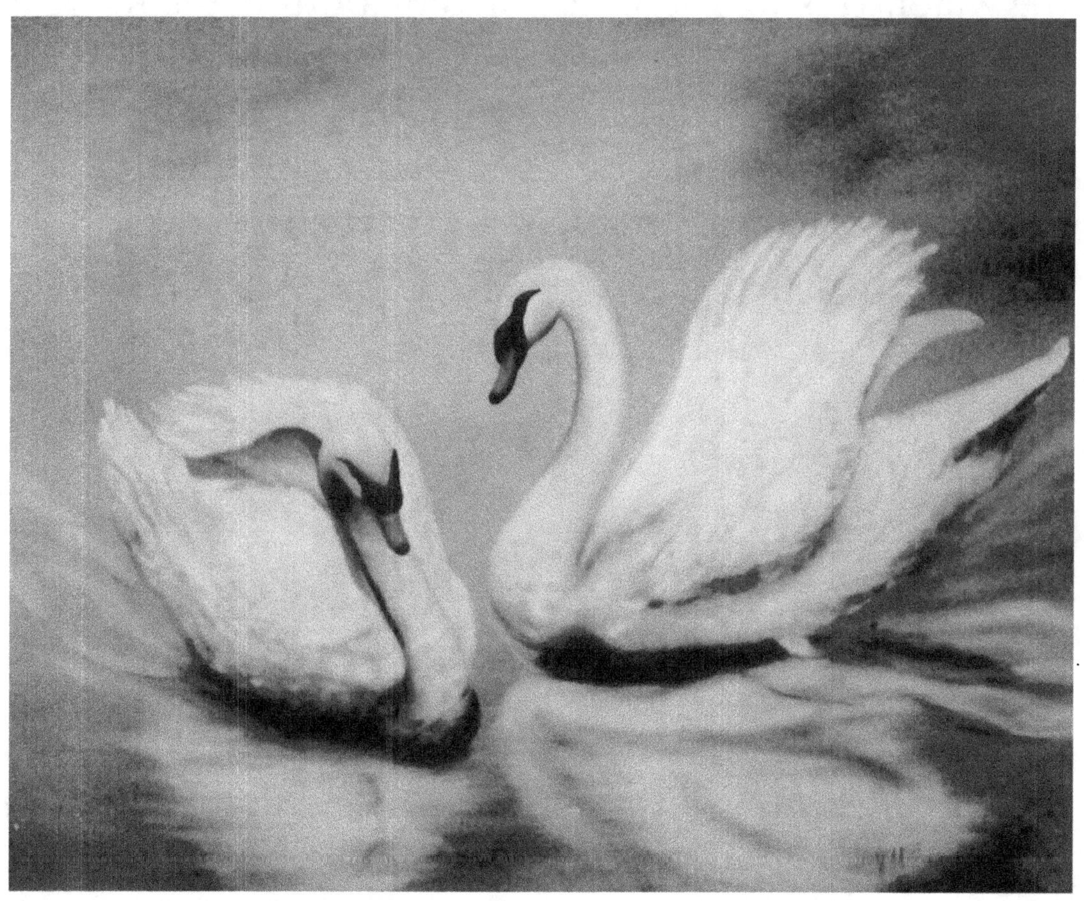

Illustration 54: watercolor

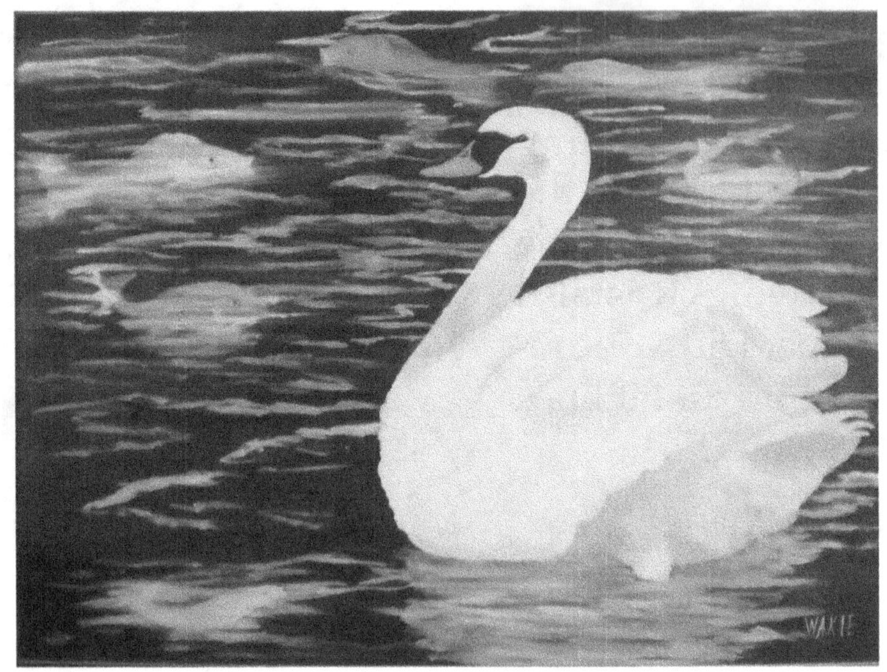

Illustration 55: *Swan Swimming*, oil

The swan is swimming on top of the water, but the fish appear to be under the water. This was accomplished by putting the reflections on top of the fish and not on the swan.

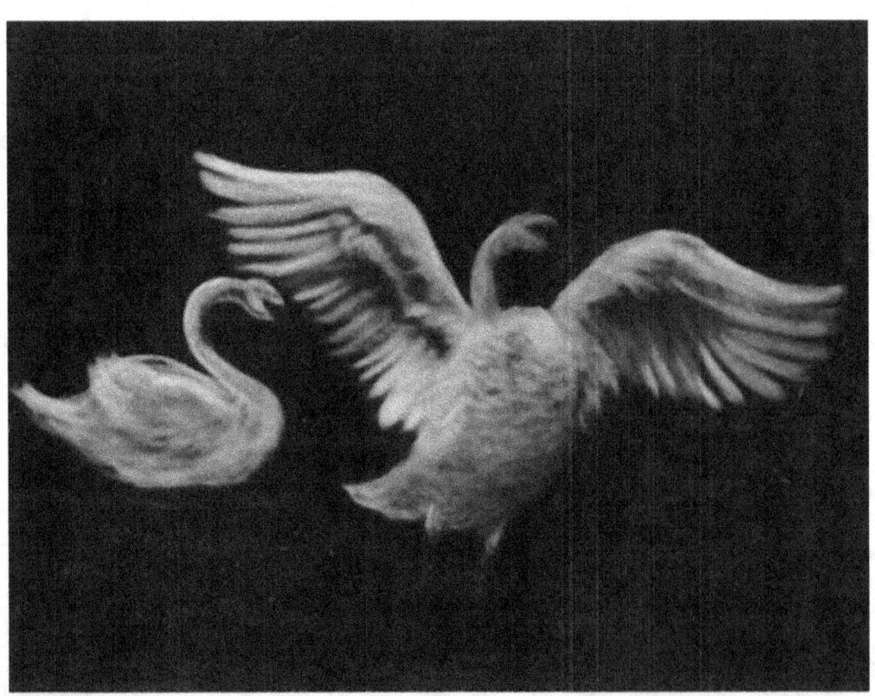

Illustration 56: soft pastels on black pastel paper

FLOWERS FROM TEARDROPS

Bearded Iris

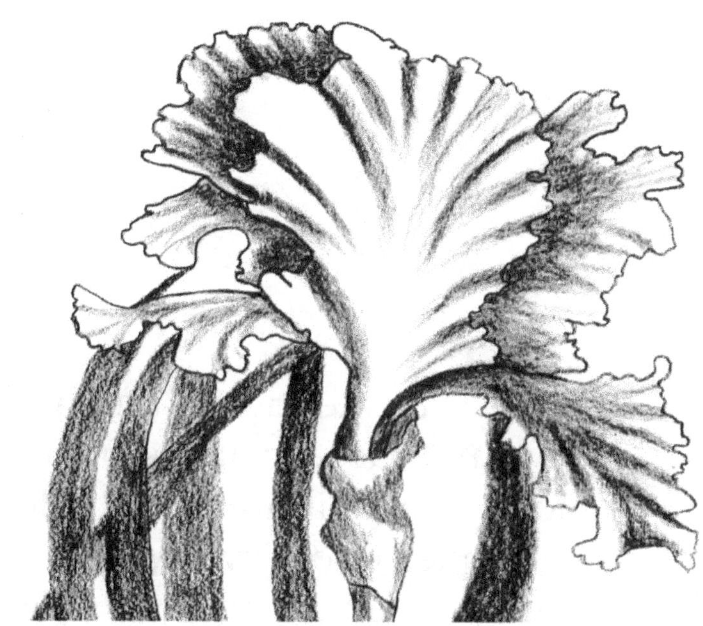

The Bearded Iris naturally has teardrop-shaped petals. Three of the petals appear as teardrops. Draw them lightly.

Illustration 57

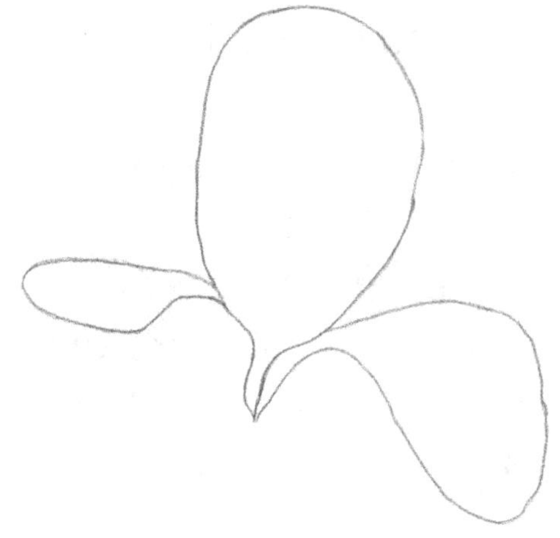

Illustration 58

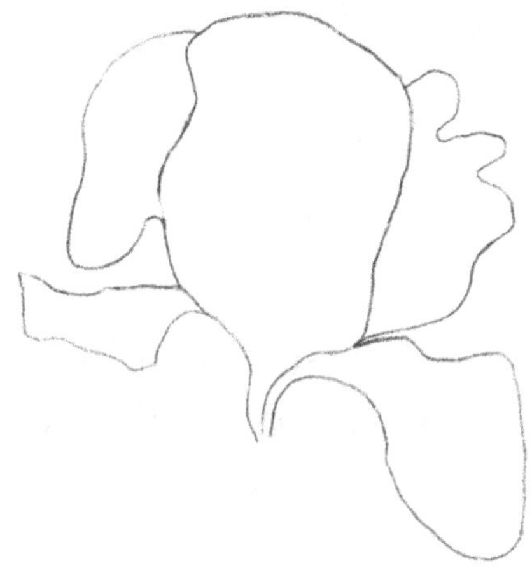

Illustration 59

You can only see parts of five petals. That is all you will draw. There are actually six, but only five are visible to you.

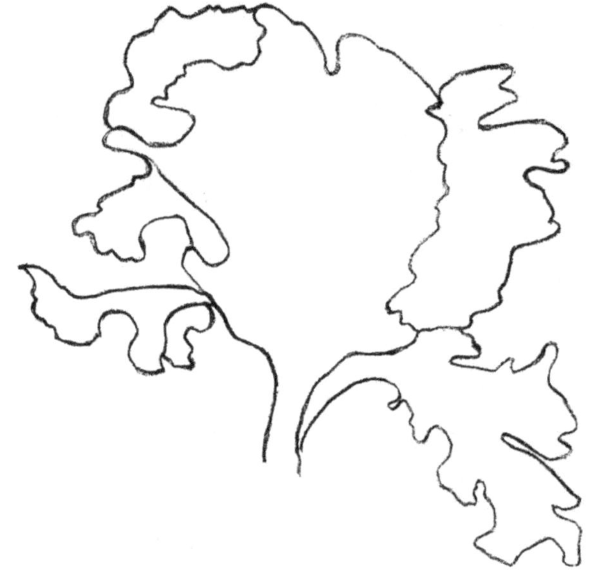

Give the petals a ruffled shape and as much flow or rhythm as you can. Note the two petals that were added last were sticking out from behind other petals.

Illustration 60

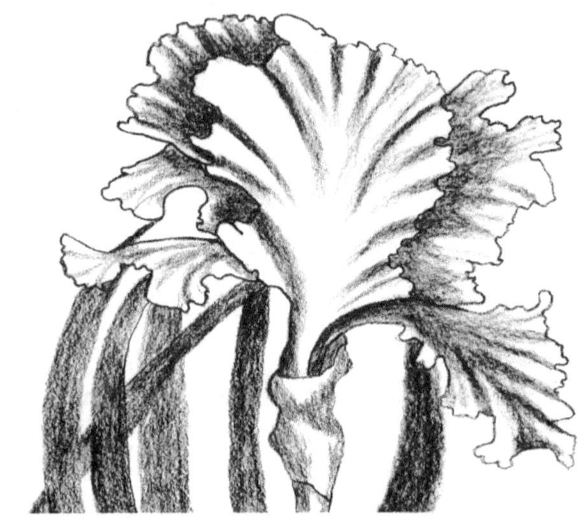

Illustration 61

Pay special attention to the shading. Anytime a petal is behind another petal, it must be shaded as it comes into view. When you ruffled the edges, you drew out and in, or up and down. I will call these hills and valleys. You will need to shade the valleys.

Also, the shading will go toward its source of strength. See how the curves in the petals give a certain rhythm to the whole flower? See how the shading helps that rhythm come to life? This is about drawing, but if you plan to paint it, do not shade it with a pencil. You will do that with paint.

Put blades, stem, and calyx on the iris. The calyx is that part which appears to join the stem and flower together. Actually, it is an onion-like skin that wraps the bud until the blossom comes forth. It stays on the stem.

This project was done without a specific light source because I want-
ed you to get the shading concept without light. This will help you to
understand the natural dips and the natural growth pattern.

Look at the following paintings of iris and see how differently they
are done.

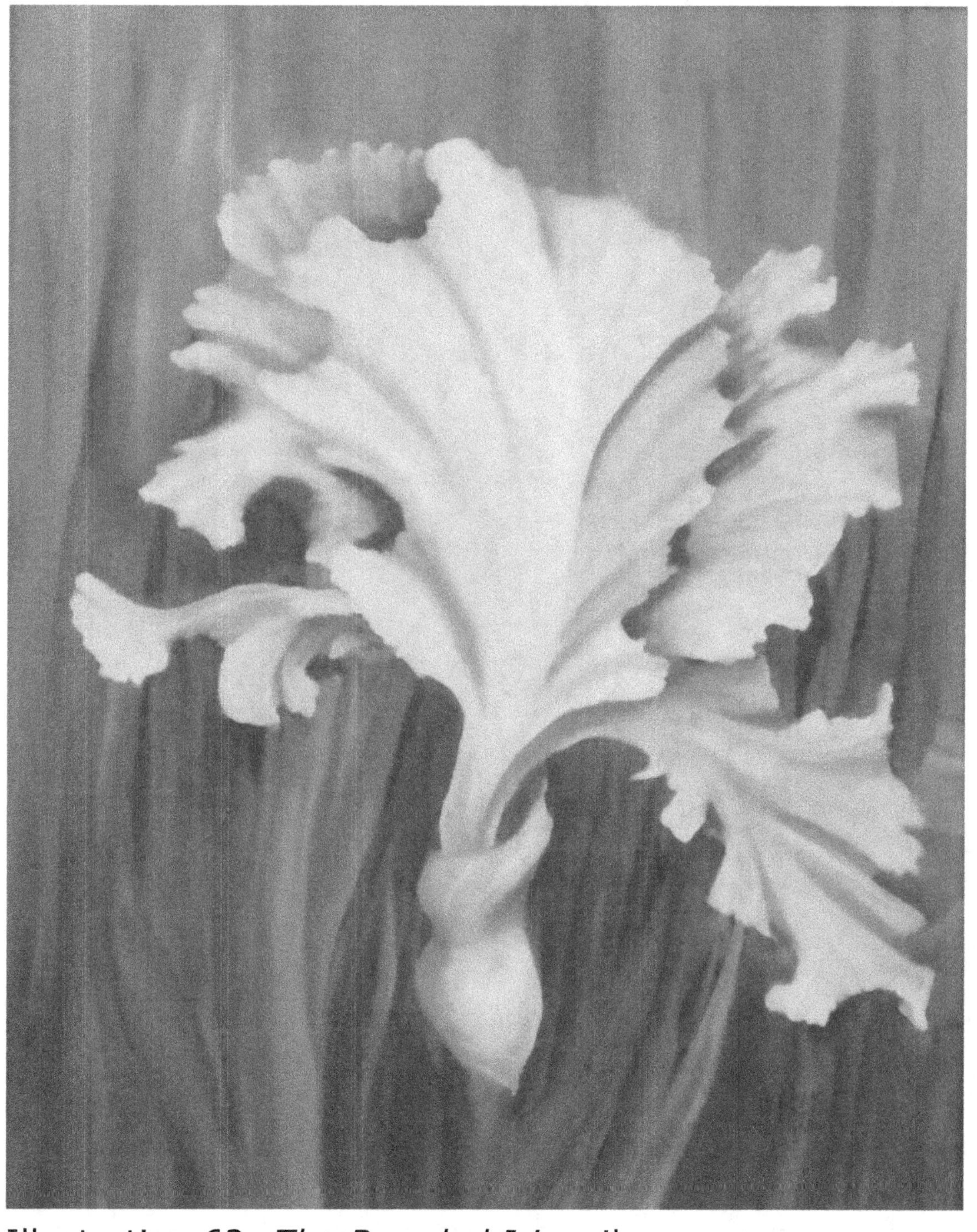

Illustration 62: *The Bearded Iris*, oil

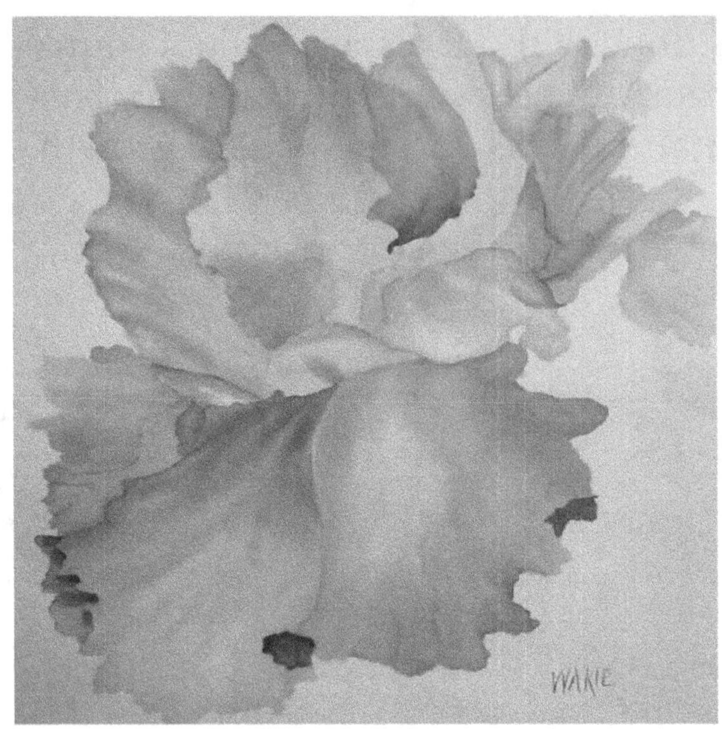

Illustration 63: *Majestic Iris*, watercolor

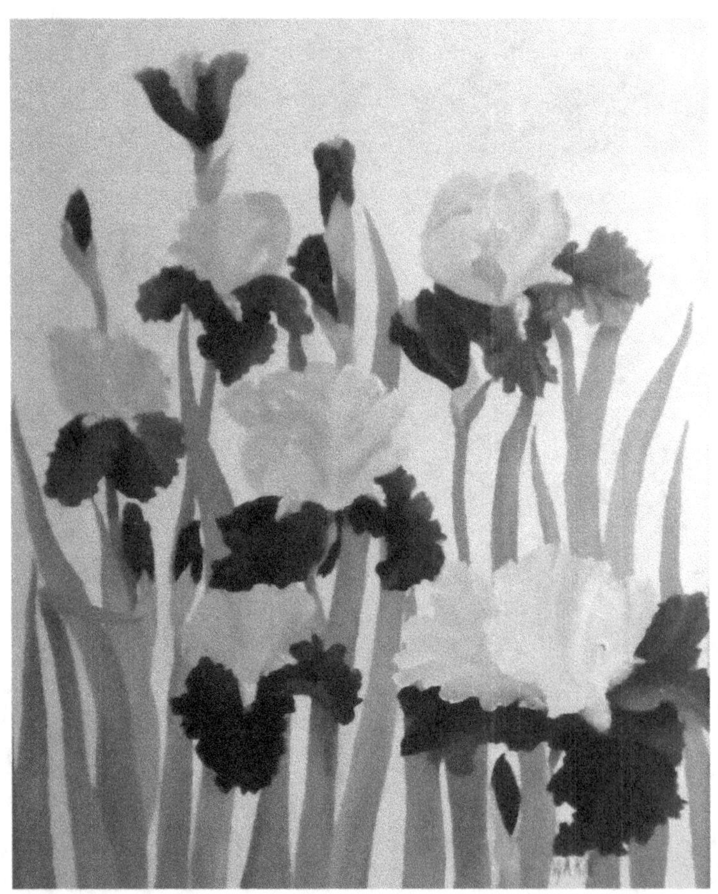

Illustration 64: *Fluttering Iris Garden*, oil

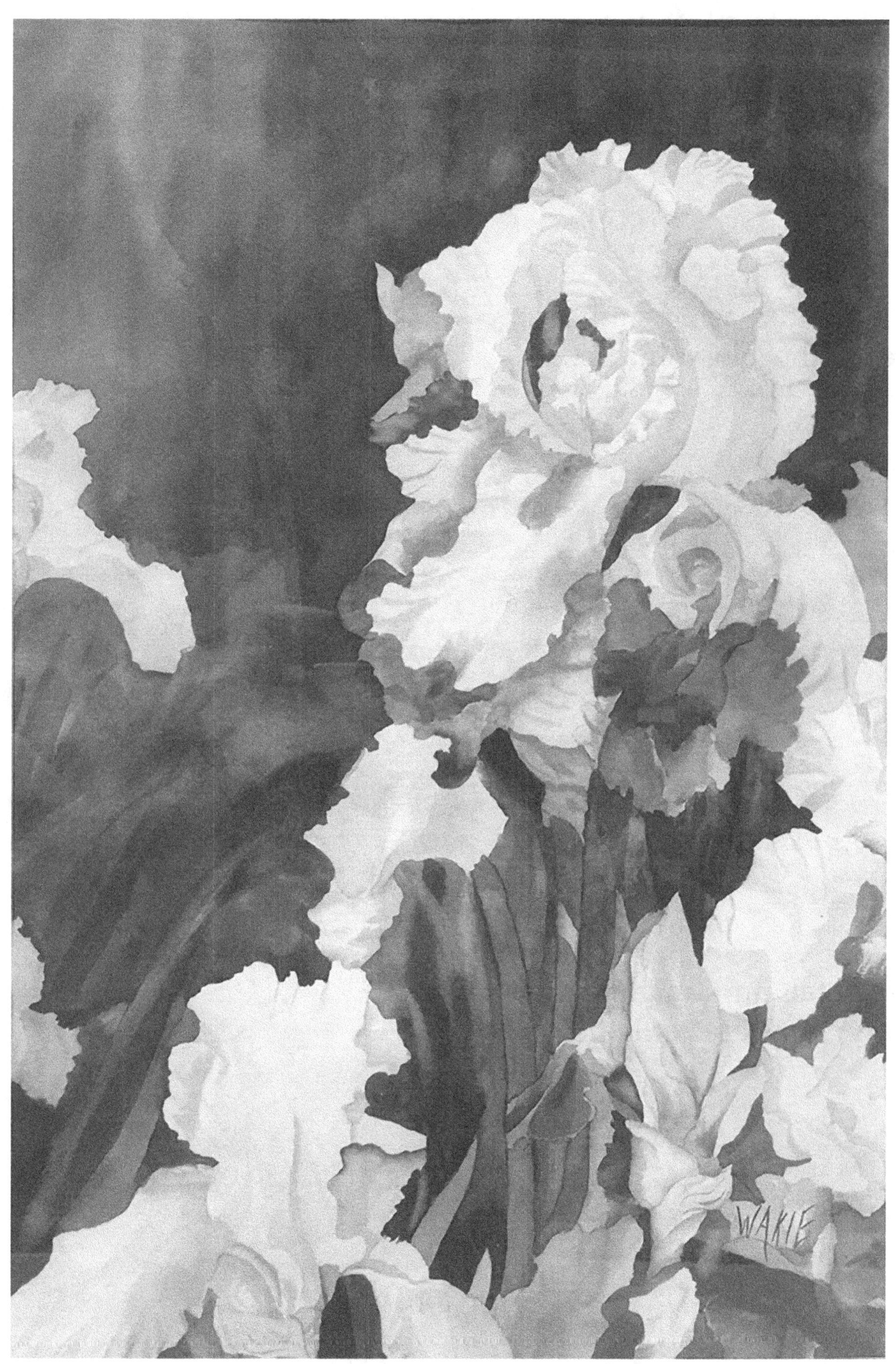

Illustration 65: *Just a Touch of Purple*, watercolor

Orchid

This orchid has a sunken place in the blossom. Let's draw it.

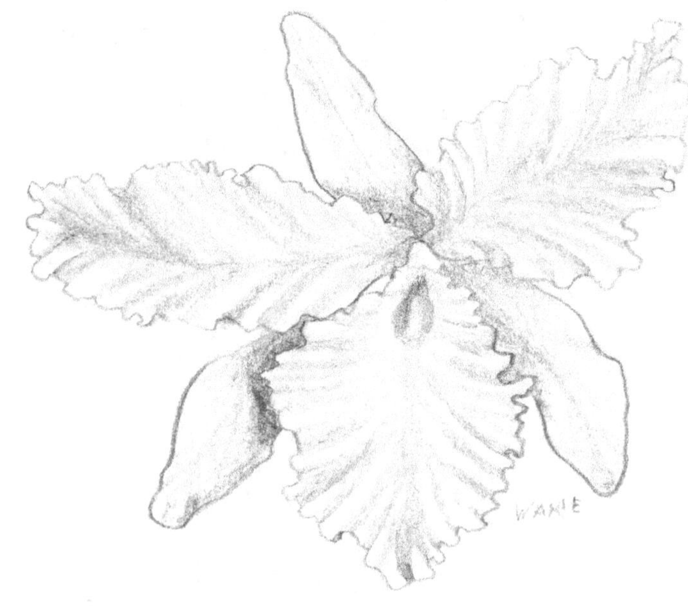

Illustration 66

Three petals are straight and narrow; three are ruffled.

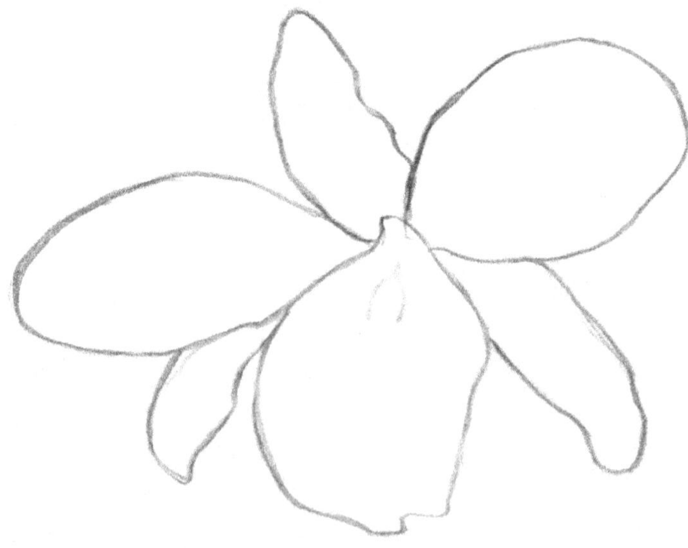

Illustration 67

Hold the pencil lightly when making the petals ruffled or they will look stiff and pointed.

Shade the valleys. We shade those petals that come from behind other petals as they appear. Remember the hills and valleys.

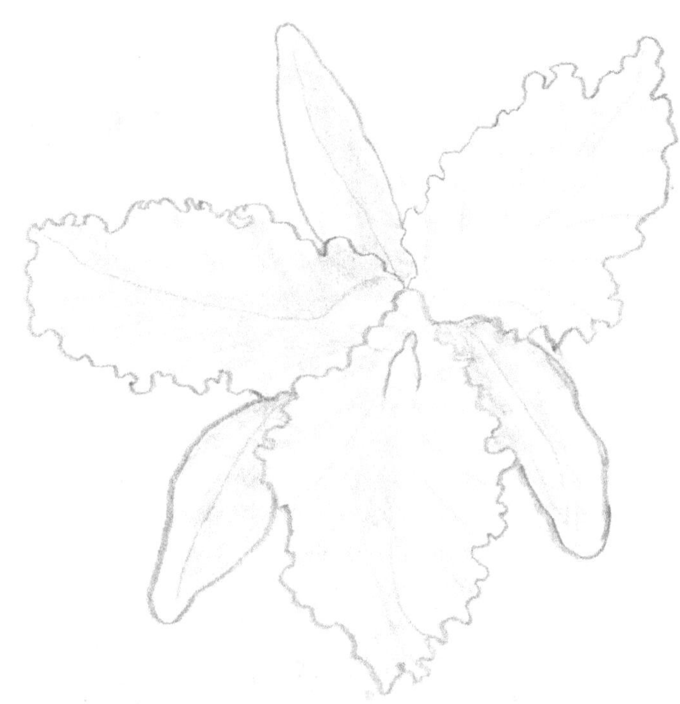

Illustration 68

Notice that the shading follows a pattern. All lines flow back to the flower's source of life, the center of the blossom. The life source flows from the stem, which proceeds from the plant, which comes from its roots. This is true of every living flower and shrub.

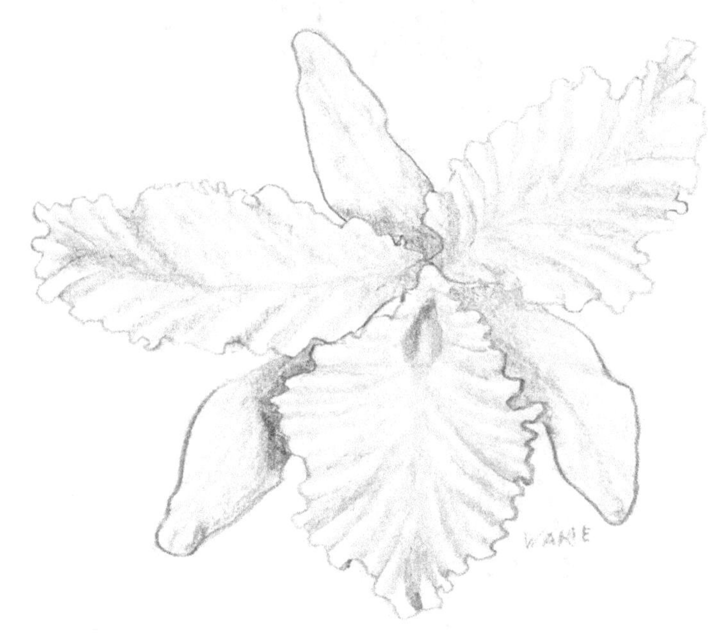

Illustration 69

TREES

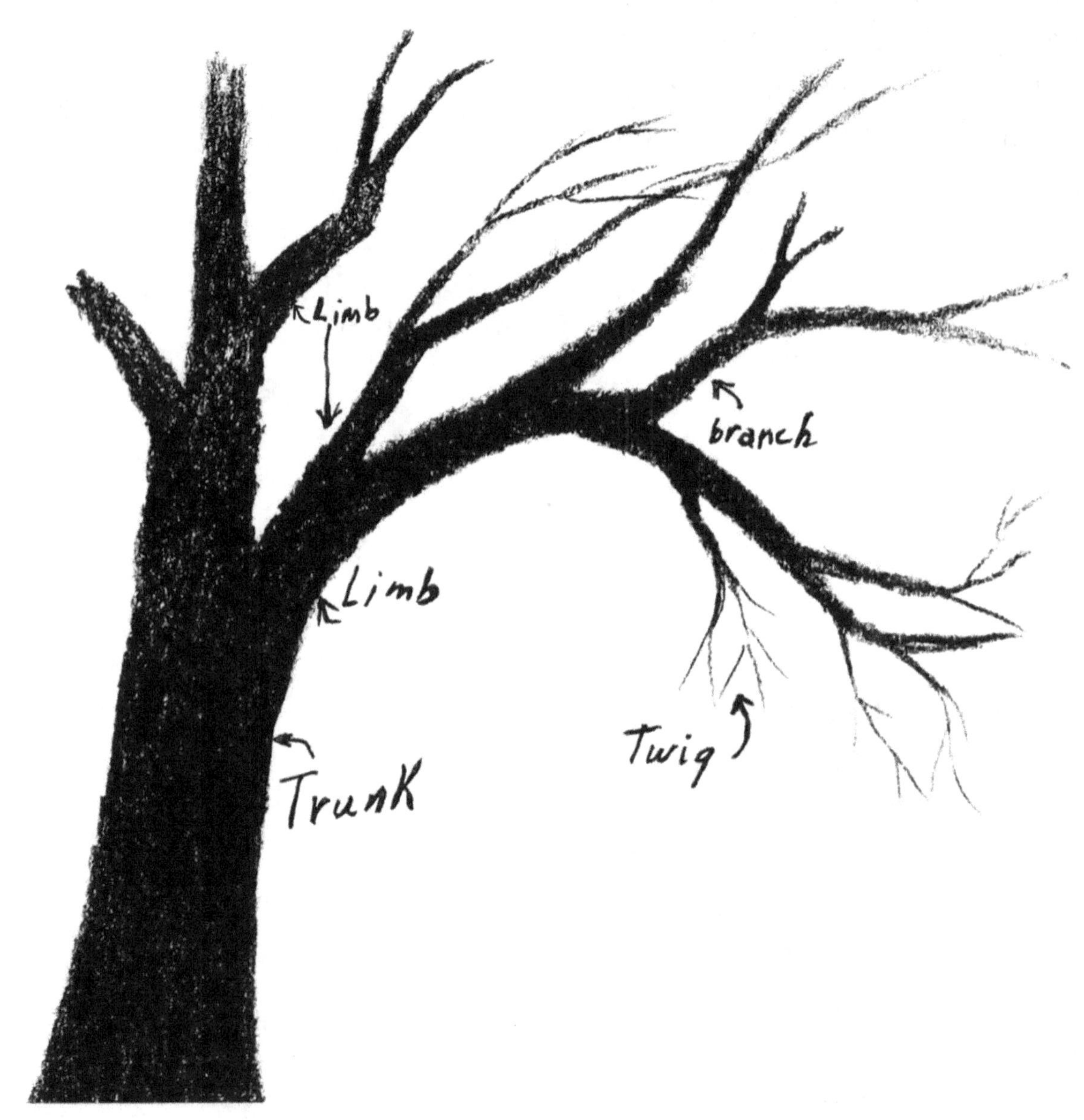

Illustration 70

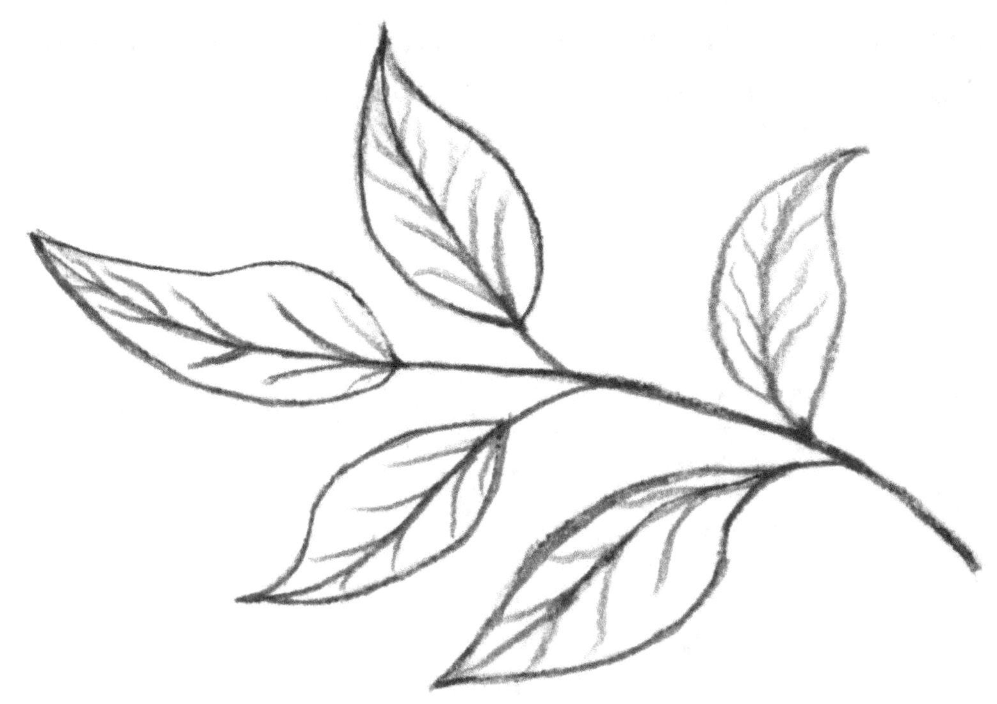

Illustration 71

We will start this series with a sprig of leaves because we can learn principles that apply to trees also. Notice that the sprig of leaves is curved. The stem of leaves grows up and out. If you start from centerline and go into the curved part of the leaf from there, the curve will look more natural. Almost without exception, everything green grows up and out from its source of strength.

Go outside with pencil in hand. With one eye closed, hold the pencil horizontally at arm's length and look at a tree. Measure the width of the tree trunk by moving your thumb along the pencil. Then measure from just above the first limb by sliding your thumb on the pencil. Now measure it above the second limb, and the third. Notice the tree trunk does not taper gradually. It only gets smaller when it subdivides to add a limb. The same is true of limbs, branches, and twigs. A twig could not hold the weight of a branch. Neither could a branch hold the weight of a limb. The trunk of the tree cannot hold the weight of any limb larger than itself. This is common sense, but it is important enough to merit mention.

To draw trees well, you need to draw different kinds of trees and lots of them. Draw the actual tree you are looking at.

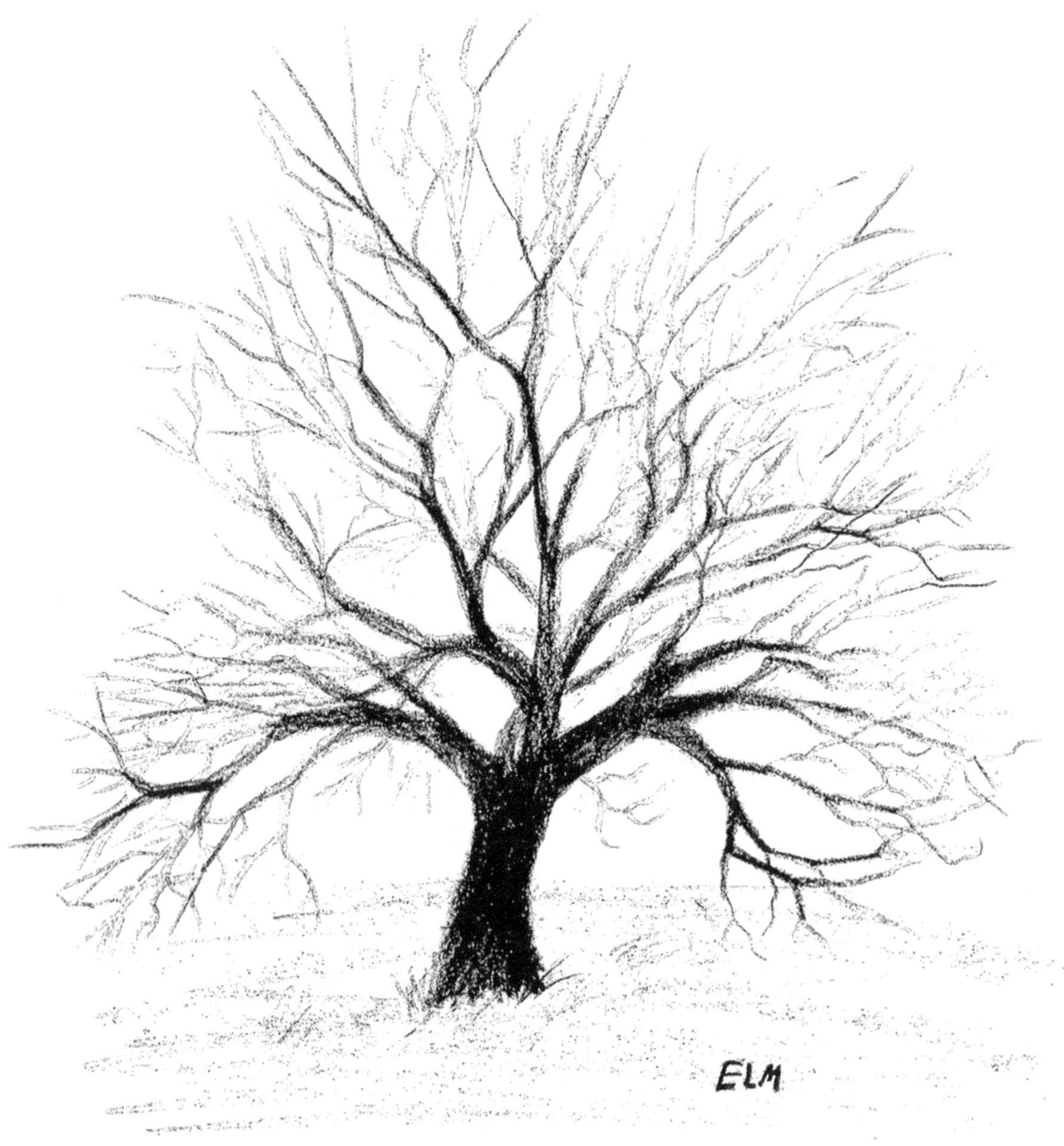

Illustration 72

This one is an elm and is a hardwood.

I drew this one bare of leaves for you to see limbs as they leave the trunk. You can see that they grow up and out.

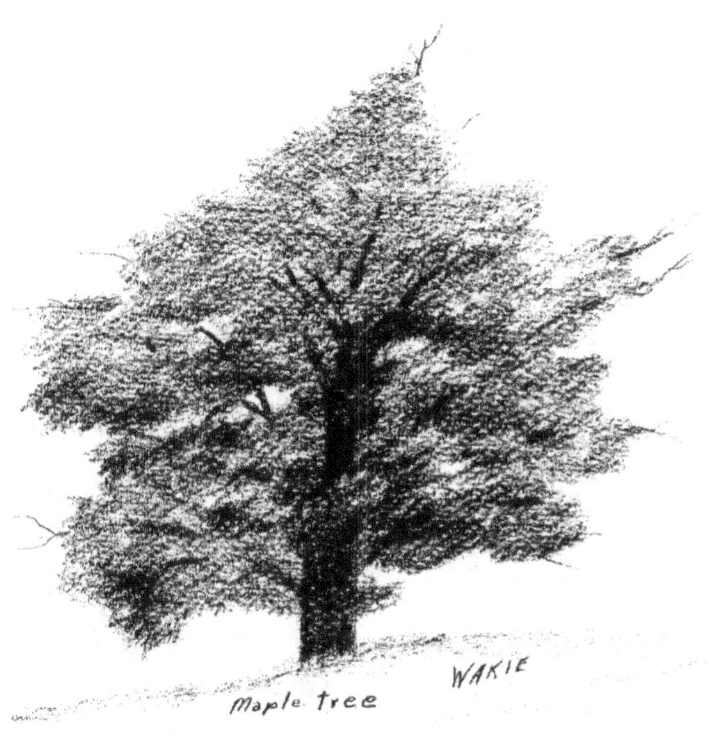

Illustration 73

This is a maple, which is also a hardwood.

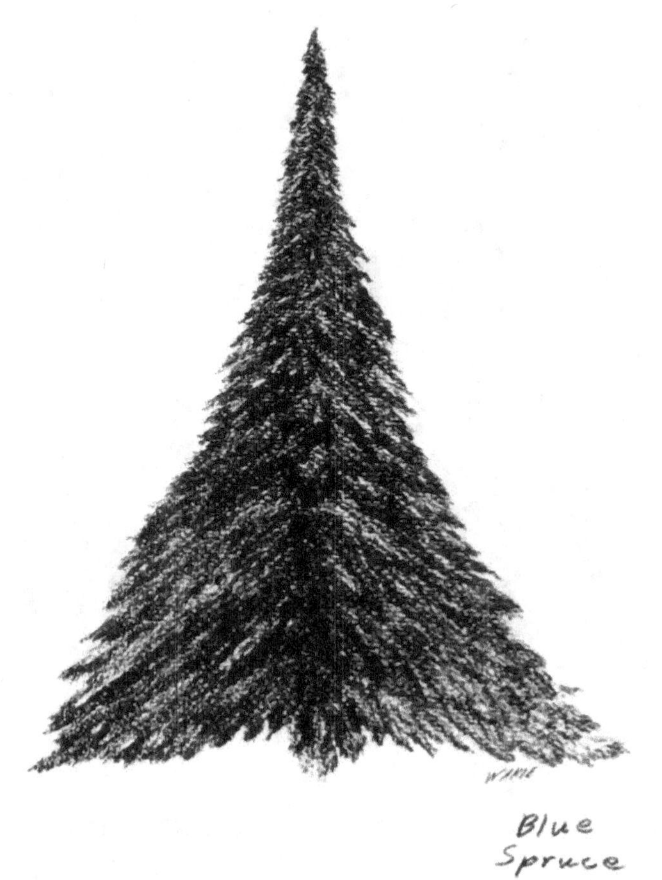

This tree is from the spruce family.

Illustration 74

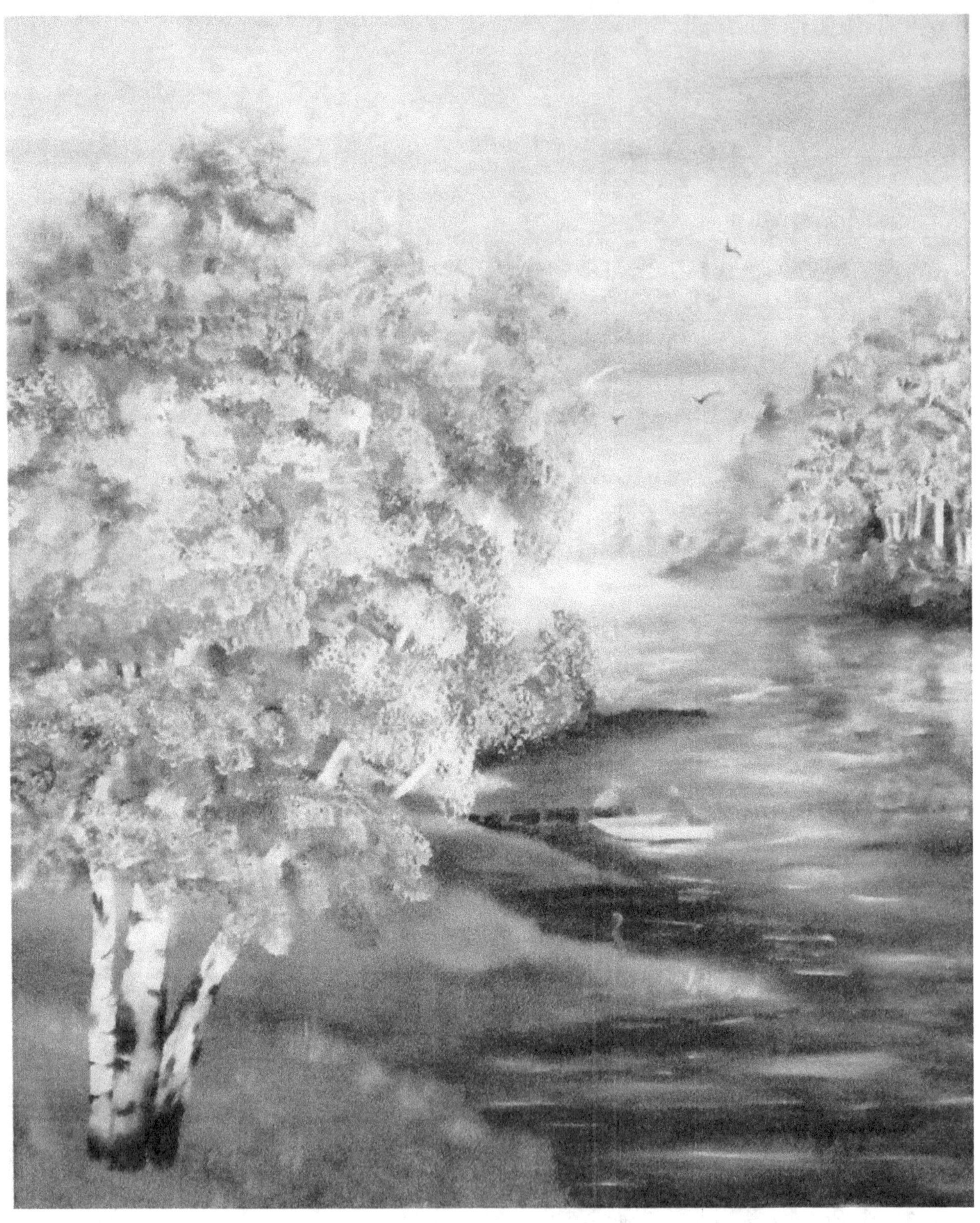

Illustration 75: *Peace at Sunrise*, oil

These trees are from the birch family. The clumps of leaves in the foreground are lighter and brighter, while those in the shade or behind
other clumps of leaves on the far side of the tree are duller and darker.

PERSPECTIVE

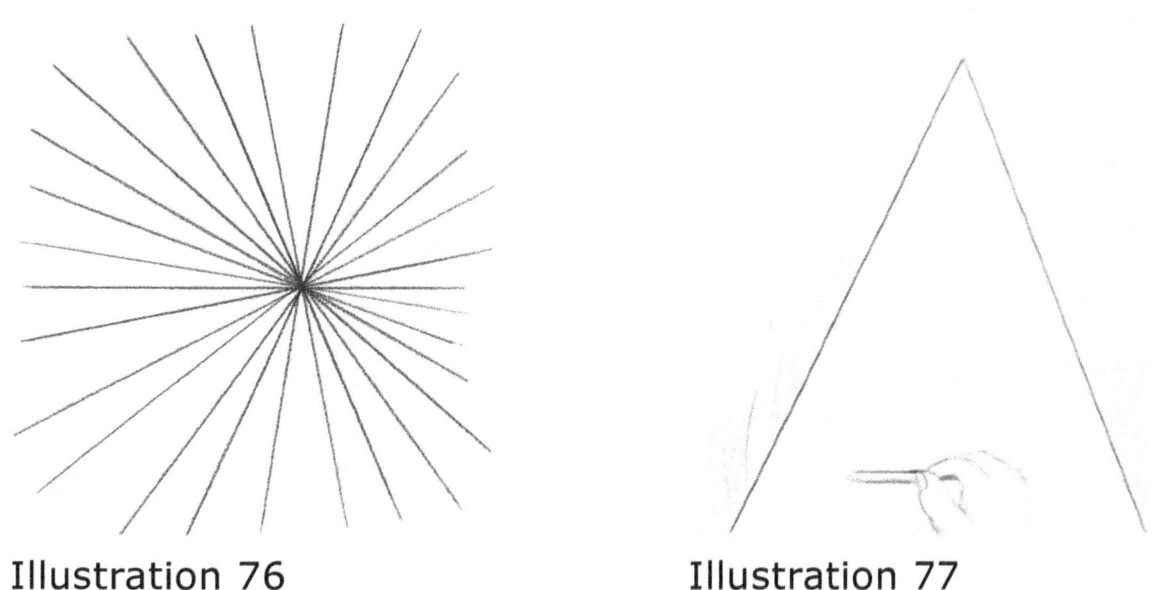

Illustration 76   Illustration 77

Illustration 76 represents the lines from the beginning of whatever you are drawing. You will make a dotted or broken line to the end of one of the lines. This will give a sense of depth to your drawing.

Illustration 77 is an example of measuring the road by sliding your thumb along a pencil. Take a pencil outside and look down the road, paying attention to the two edges. If the road is long enough, the two sides will appear to run together. That is the vanishing point, that point at which two parallel lines run together.

Hold the pencil at arm's length. With one eye closed and the pencil held horizontally, measure the distance between the two sides of the road. Slide your thumb back and forth on the pencil until you get a good visual. Notice the width of the road near where you are standing, according to your measurement. Continue measuring it further and further away. Do you understand? In other words, the greater distance away anything is from you, the smaller it needs to be drawn in order to appear that way.

If you have vertical poles, posts, buildings, weeds, etc., along the road, measure the heights of them as they get farther away. You will need to turn your pencil vertically.

If you put some utility poles beside the road, that will make it more interesting.

Perspective allows you to draw three-dimensional objects or landscapes on a two-dimensional piece of paper while maintaining the appearance of three dimensions.

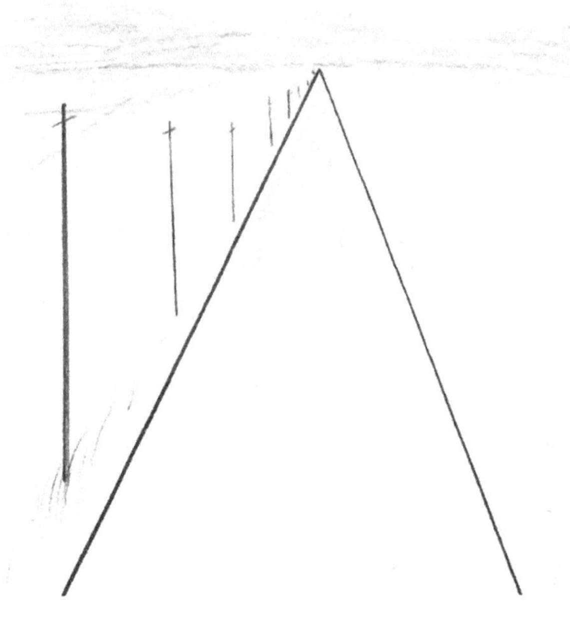

Illustration 78

The viewer's eye is directed to the focal point. We have made all the major lines pointing to it but have given him no reason to look there. There is nothing of interest to see. Let's fix that.

Now there is at least something for the viewer to see.

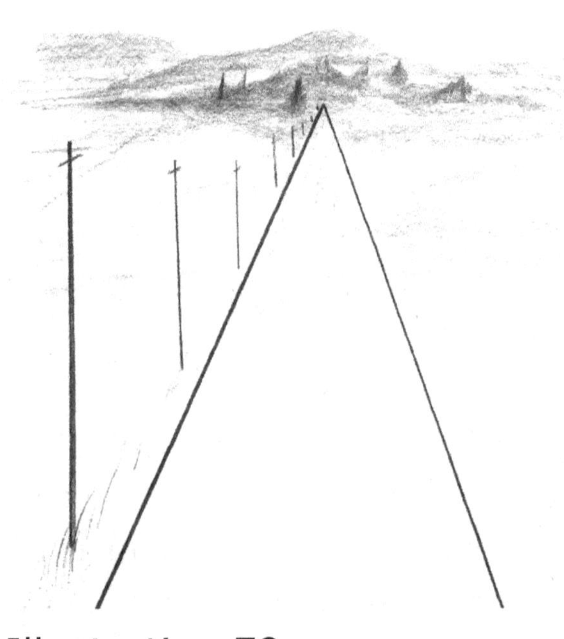

Illustration 79

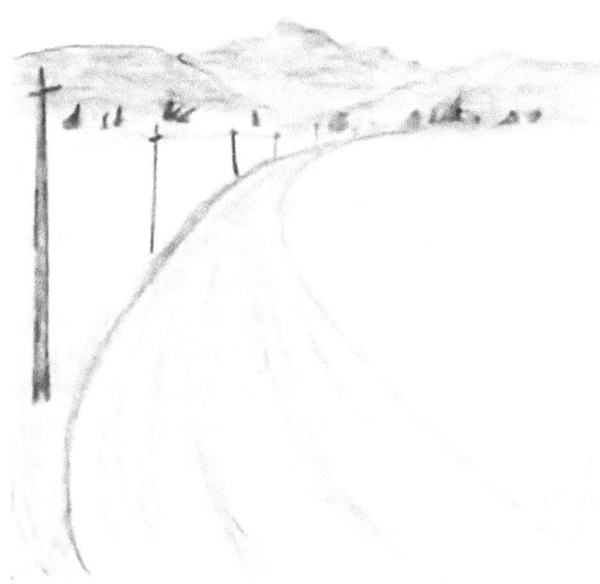

Let's make the road curve. See how it looks now? Always reward the viewer by making your point of interest something they will enjoy seeing. We are in the entertainment business.

Any indication of life makes a composition more interesting. We have curved the road and put a house at the end of the road with smoke coming out the chimney.

Illustration 80

Here is one of my paintings incorporating all of these things. See how a few details improve the composition.

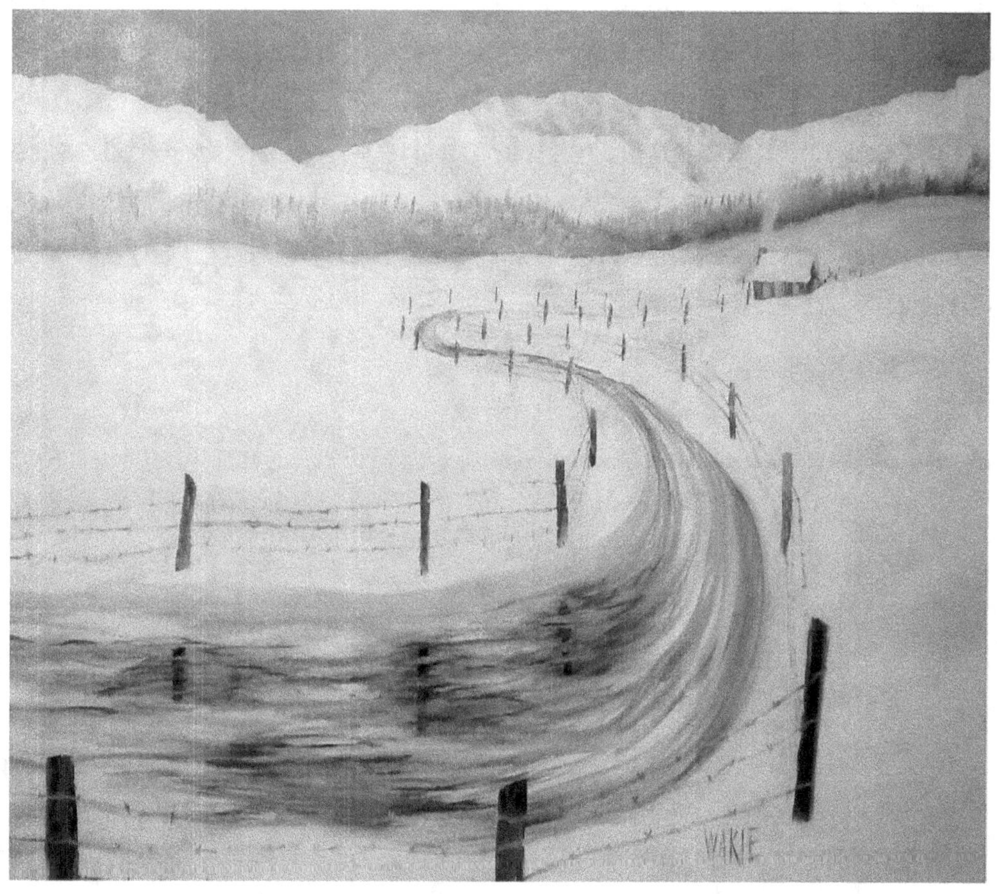

Illustration 81: *Beginning to Thaw*, oil

SQUARES & RECTANGLES

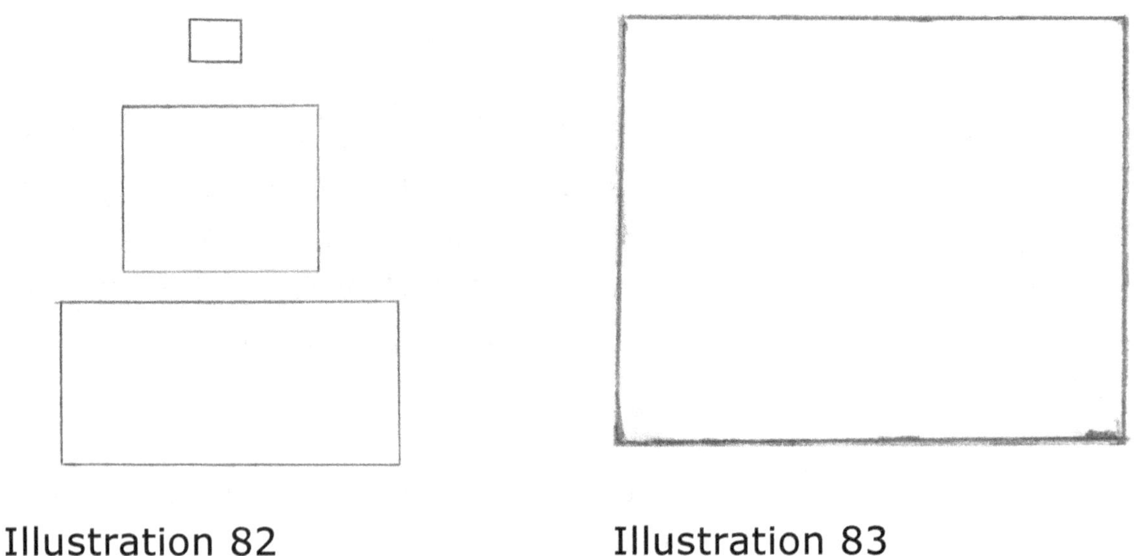

Illustration 82   Illustration 83

We can also make things of a square or a rectangle. Use a ruler for this type drawing. Draw a square and set it down. Remember, to set something down, you make a darker line at the bottom. See Illustration 83.

With a rectangle, you can make a box or a building. Draw a rectangle with a dividing line.

Illustration 84

It still lacks something, doesn't it? The illustration lacks perspective, which the shaded part needs to make it appear to have three dimensions. We will do that by adding a vanishing point, that point at which two parallel lines appear to come together.

Put a vanishing point as far right as the page will allow. With a ruler, draw a broken line from the top and the bottom of the dividing line to the vanishing point. This will give the right side of the rectangle the appearance of being further away.

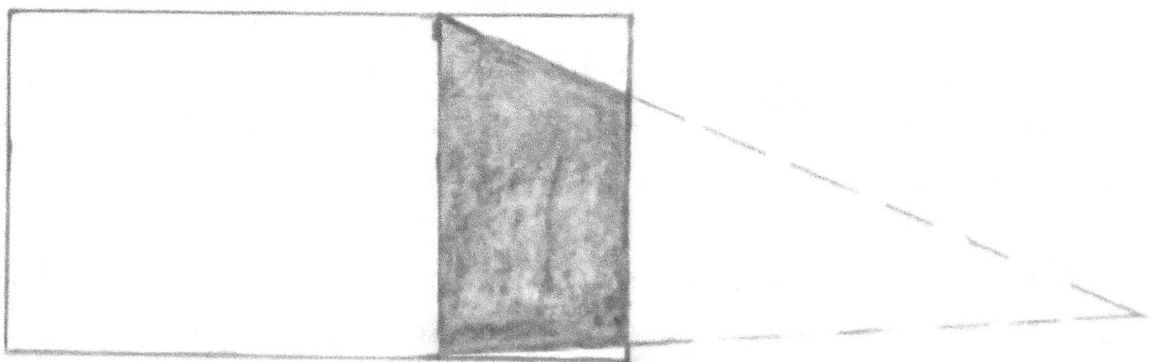

Illustration 85

On the right side of the rectangle, shade inside the broken lines from the dividing line to the right end of the rectangle. Erase the two broken lines from the right side of the rectangle, as well as the top and bottom right corners.

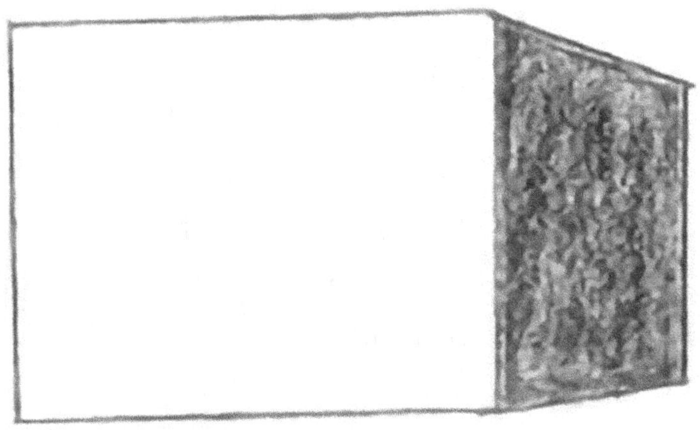

We have what appears to be a three-dimensional shape. We did that with help of the vanishing point. That is what perspective is about.

Illustration 86

You can start with a rectangle and turn it into a box, building, house, or even animals.

Flat-Roof Building

Take a pencil and sketch pad outside. Find a rectangular building with a flat roof. Line yourself up with the corner of the building so you can see two sides. Go about one-half block or more from that corner, which will be the corner closest to you.

Draw a vertical line in the middle of the page, and we will use that for the corner of the building. Put a vanishing point on each side, about as far as space will allow. This vertical line will be called the centerline from this point in this building project.

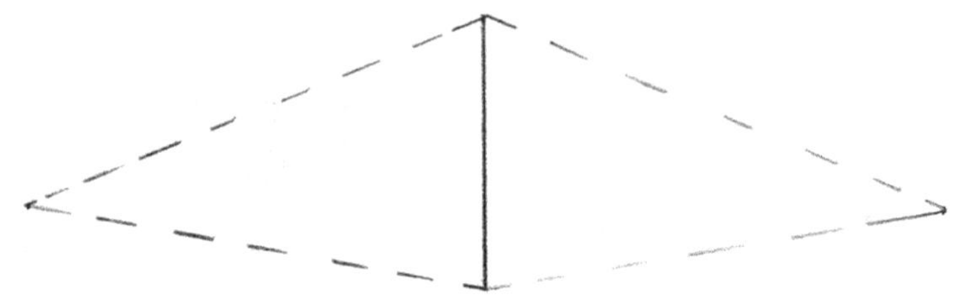

With a ruler, draw broken lines from the top and bottom of the centerline to the right and the left vanishing points.

Illustration 87

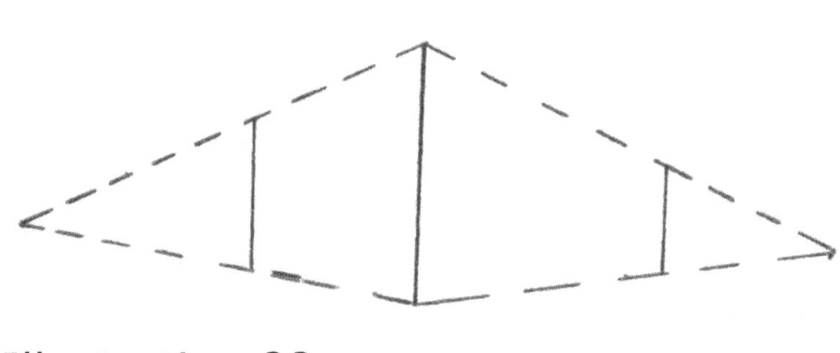

Measure out a distance from the centerline, as far as you estimate the ends of the building to be. Remember to use a pencil for measuring. Draw a vertical line between the broken lines on both sides as indicated in Illustration 88.

Illustration 88

We will keep the same vanishing points in place for the rest of the drawing. Making things seem further away is simply a matter of perspective. It is necessary to make what you wish to appear far away, smaller, and duller or darker. And to make things look closer, they need to be lighter and brighter. Keep this idea in your mind.

All horizontal lines on the left of the centerline go to the left vanishing point. All horizontal lines to the right of the centerline go to the right vanishing point. Remember to always draw the broken lines lightly; they will all need to be erased later.

Go about one third of the way down on the centerline. Mark that point. From that point, draw a broken line from the centerline to each of the vanishing points. This line will show the location for the top of the doors and windows. Use a ruler for this type of drawing.

On the left side of the building, draw a broken-line X from top left to bottom right, and from top right to bottom left. The center of the X is optically the center of the end of the building.

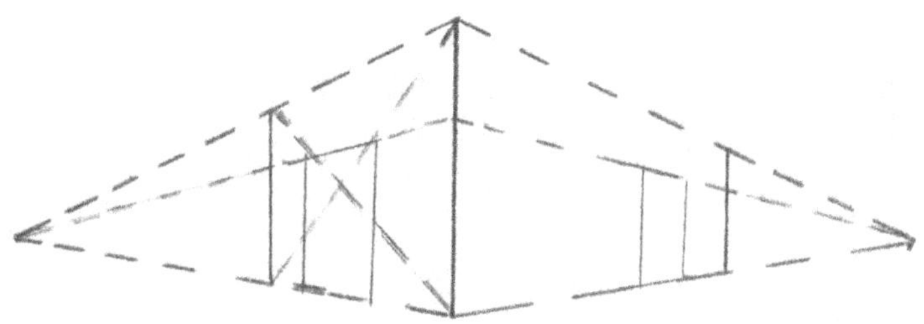

Illustration 89

Place the door in the center of the end of the building. Use the second line from the top of the building as a guide for the top of doors.

Make solid lines of all broken lines necessary for the shape of the building. Erase all remaining broken lines.

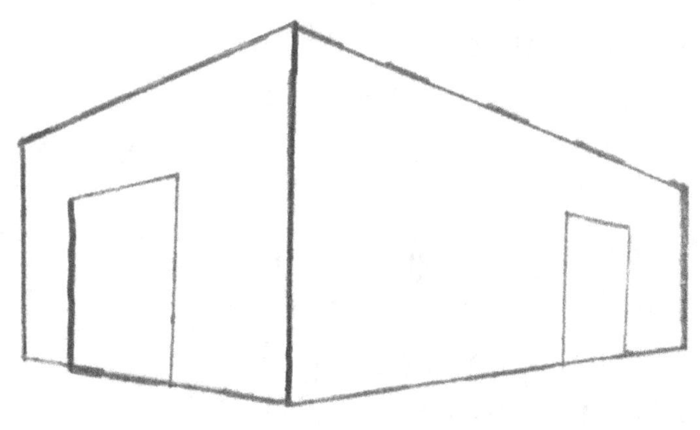

Illustration 90

You have drawn a straight flat-top building.

Pitched Roof Building

Here is what one house with a pitched roof looks like. Let's draw this house.

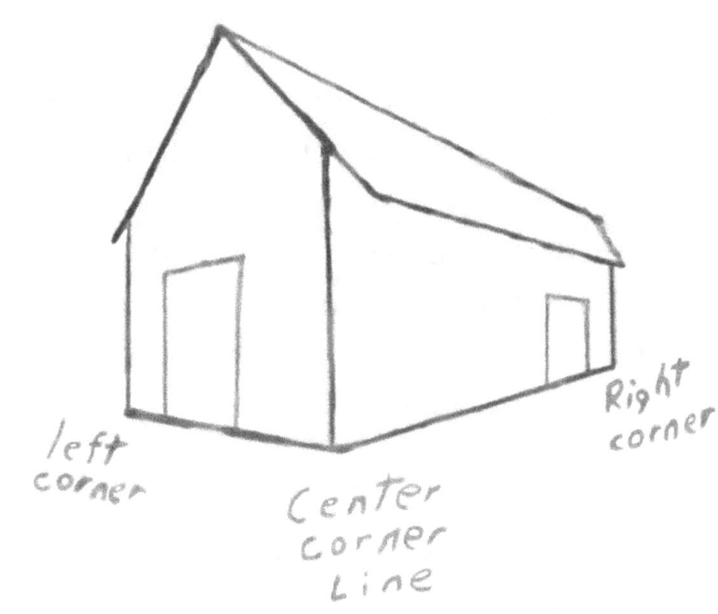

Illustration 91

Illustration 92 is a copy of Illustration 89. If you need to, look back at the illustrations and instructions for a flat-top building. Then pick up at this point.

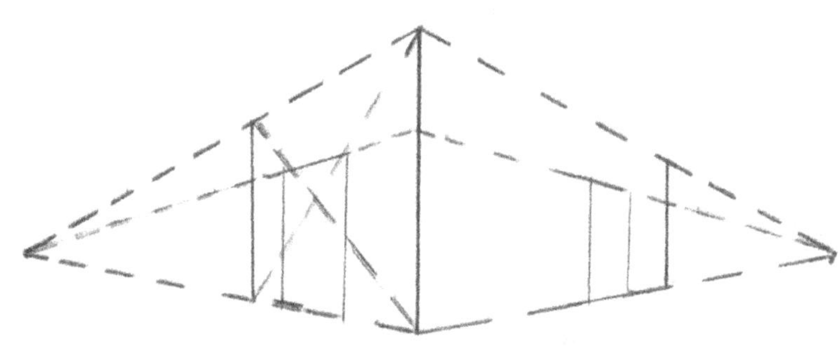

Illustration 92

Draw a broken line straight down from two or more inches above the top of the building where the X is, and go through the center of the X to the bottom of the building.

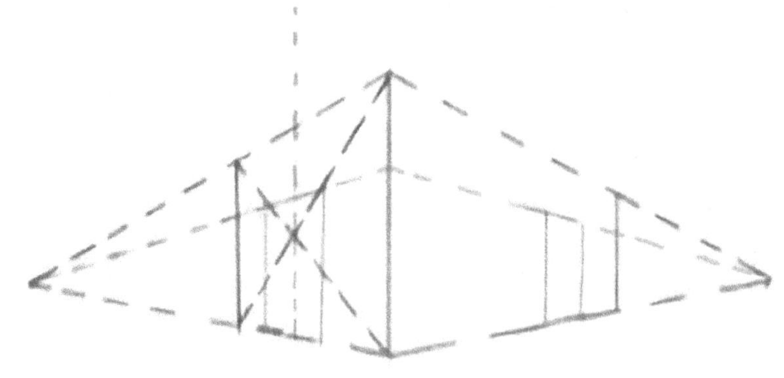

Illustration 93

In Illustration 94, the top of the original flat-top building is Line 1. The original line used as a guide for the tops of the doors is Line 3.

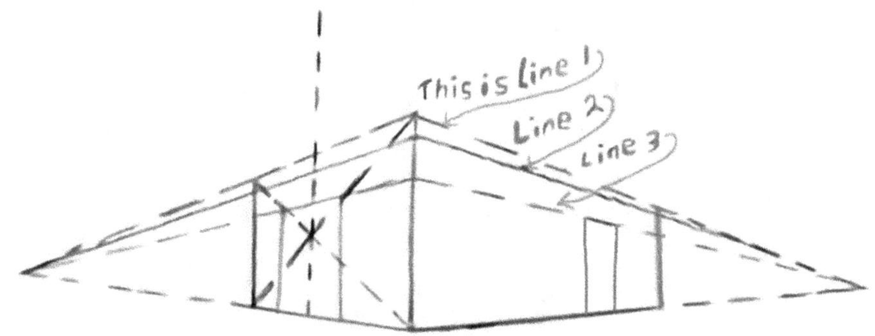

Illustration 94

Let's draw Line 2. Put a mark about one third of the way down from the centerline between Line 1 and Line 3. From the mark, draw Line 2 to the right and left vanishing points.

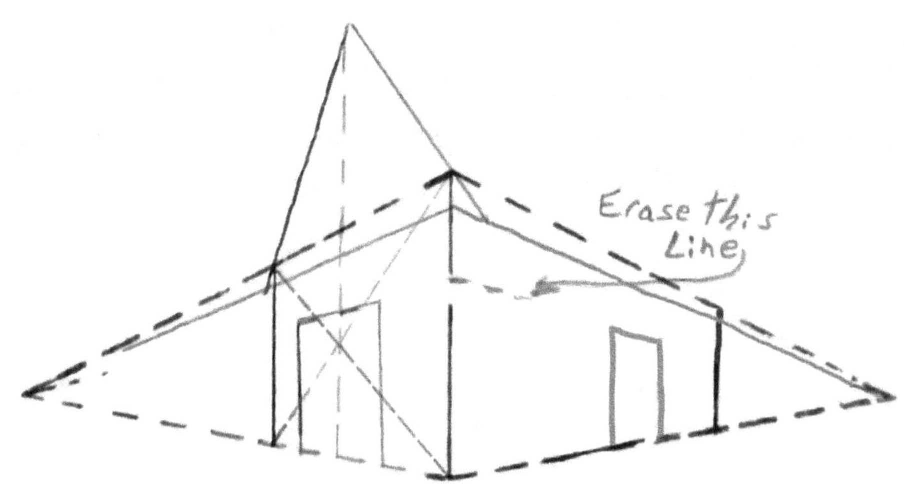

Illustration 95

Erase Line 3. Now, let's draw the pitch of the roof (an inverted *V*). With a ruler, draw a line on the right side from the top of the broken vertical line through Line 1 at the corner of the building to Line 2. Notice it goes past what was the top of the building. Draw another line on the left side from the peak to Line 2, making the left side of the inverted *V*. It also went past what was the top of the old building. This allows for an overhang.

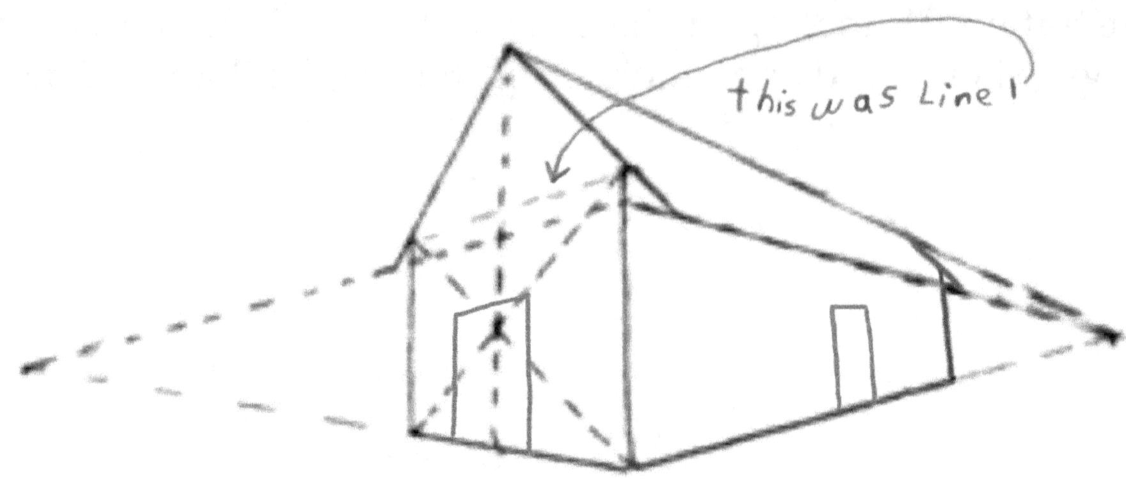

Illustration 96

Draw a line from the peak to the right vanishing point. Erase Line 1. Be careful not to erase part of the right end of the building. It still goes up to where Line 1 was.

The right end of the roof of the building is simple. Lay the ruler along the right side of the inverted *V*, and slide it, without changing its angle, until it reaches the top of the right end of the building. Draw the end of the roof there, going all the way to Line 2.

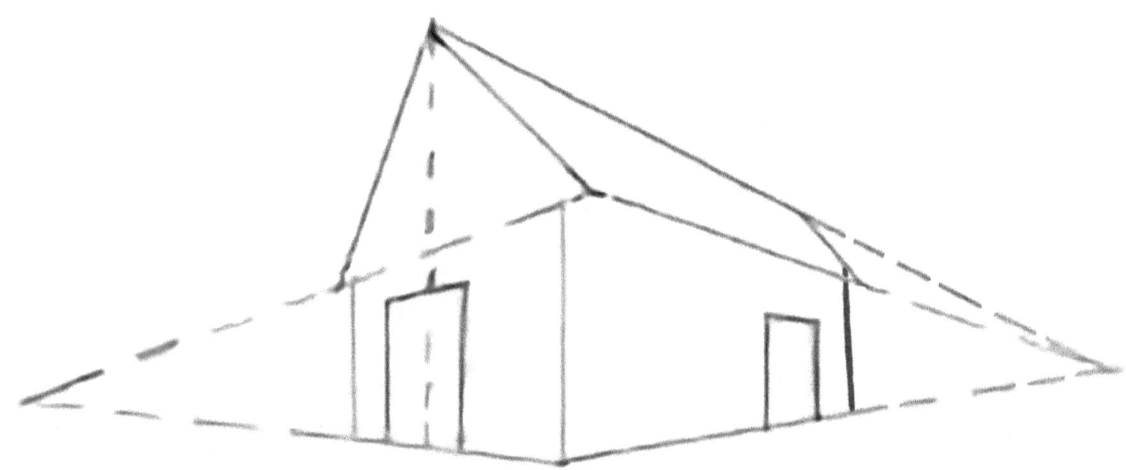

Illustration 97

Make solid lines of the broken lines that are necessary to form the building. Erase all the leftover broken lines that are not part of the building.

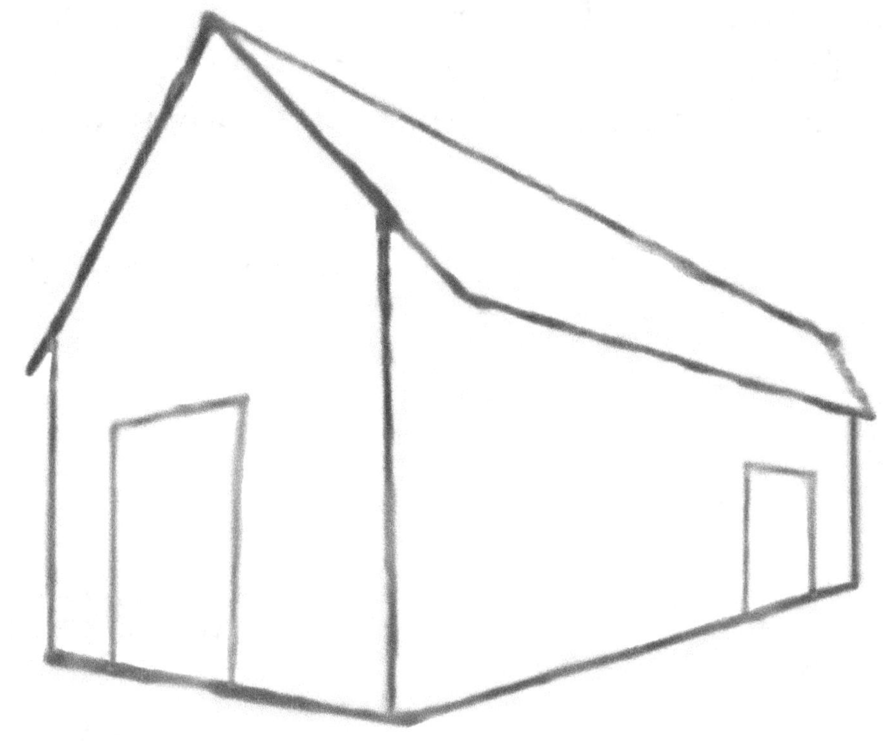

Illustration 98

You now have a finished building with a pitched roof.

The knowledge you have gained will keep you from drawing a lop-sided building.

When you take time to measure and draw the necessary lines, you will be able to draw anything.

We only used two-point perspective in this drawing. If you really want to know how to draw a building, you will want to take a course in drafting or architectural drawing. You can start with a rectangle and draw a barn, a house, or any number of things. You are in control. Whatever you can visualize, you can draw. Try it. Close your eyes and try to visualize a shape. Then, with eyes open, make something of it.

A drawing or painting of a house needs to look used and lived in, or deserted, to look more interesting. If it is an old building, it may have a sagging roof, but you must have the four corners structurally correct.

Here are some other buildings painted, using what you have just learned. This first one is a very old, abandoned barn. You can tell by the missing doors, the rusted roof, the broken-down rock silo, and tall weeds.

This barn just has a familiar look. It is not an exact rendering, but it helps to know how to draw it.

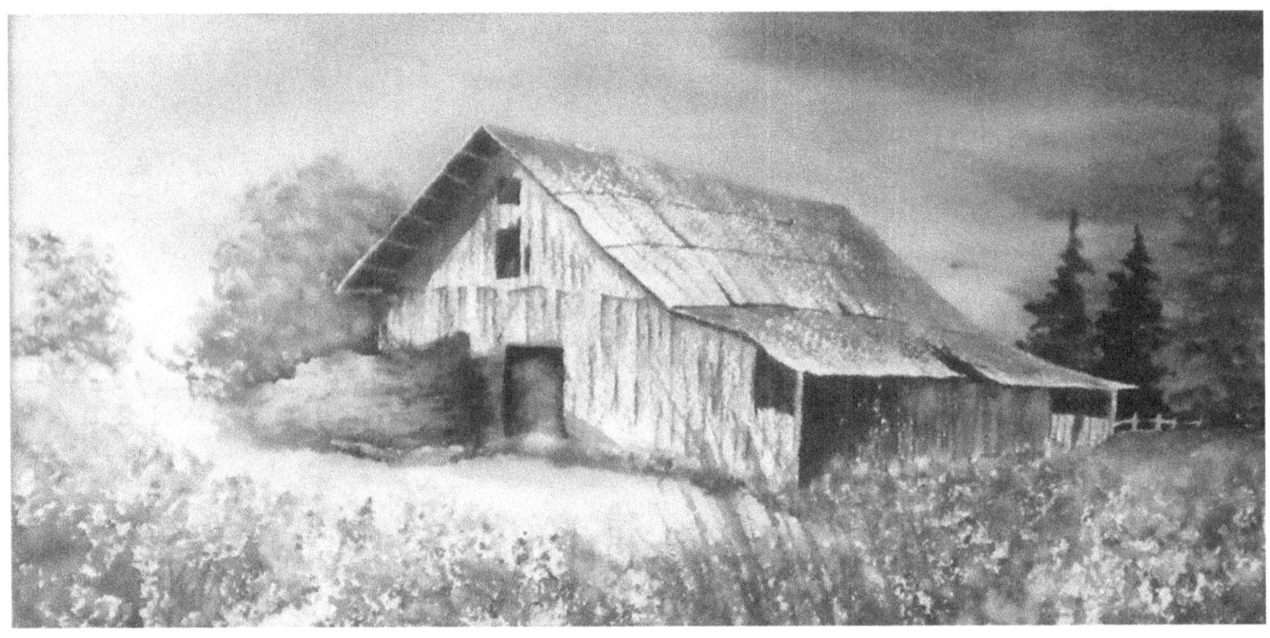

Illustration 99: *Barn with Silo*, watercolor

Find a house to sketch. Set up and do it on site. It will be fun, and you will learn so much from this experience.

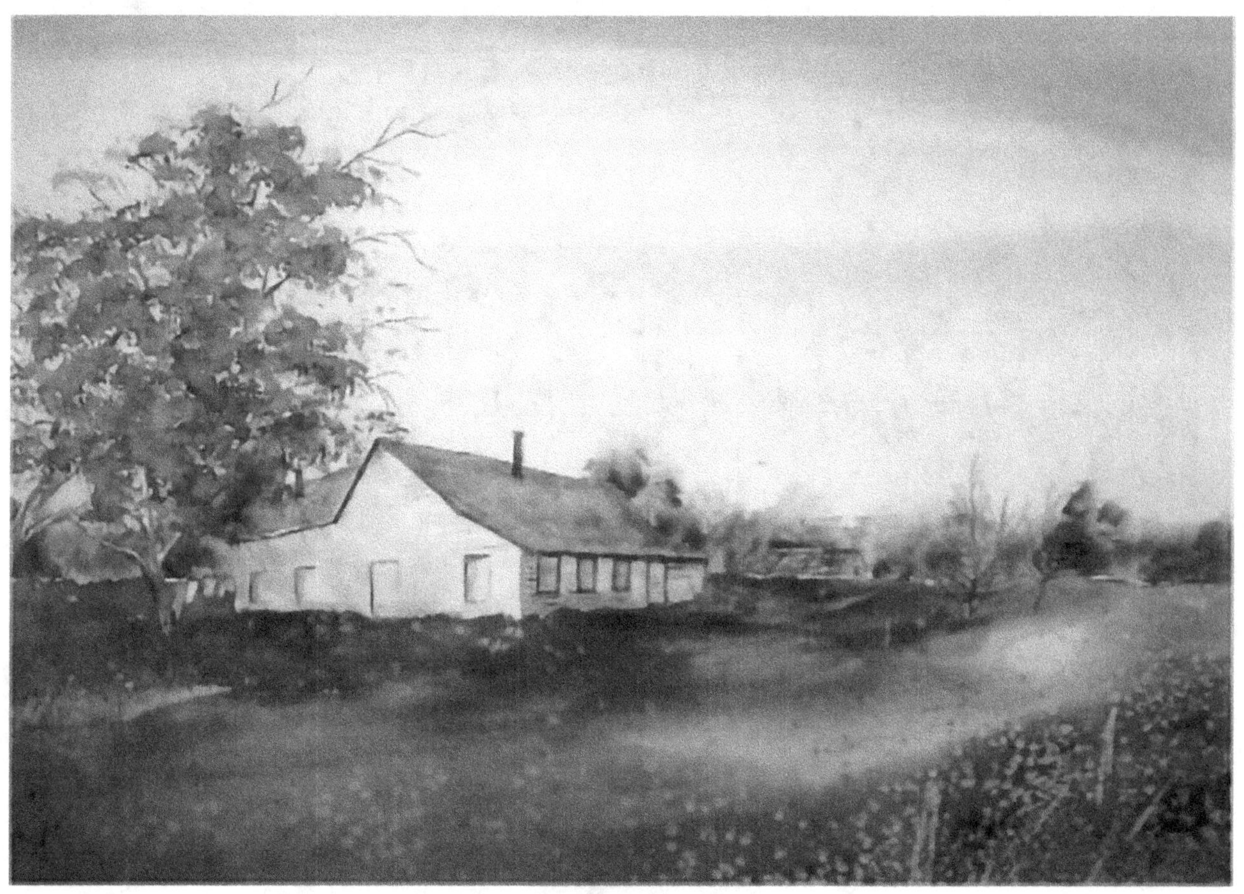

Illustration 100: *Washday*, watercolor

This sketch of an old store front was done on site with ink and brushes.
It was a cold, wet day, but we were bundled up. It was so much fun.

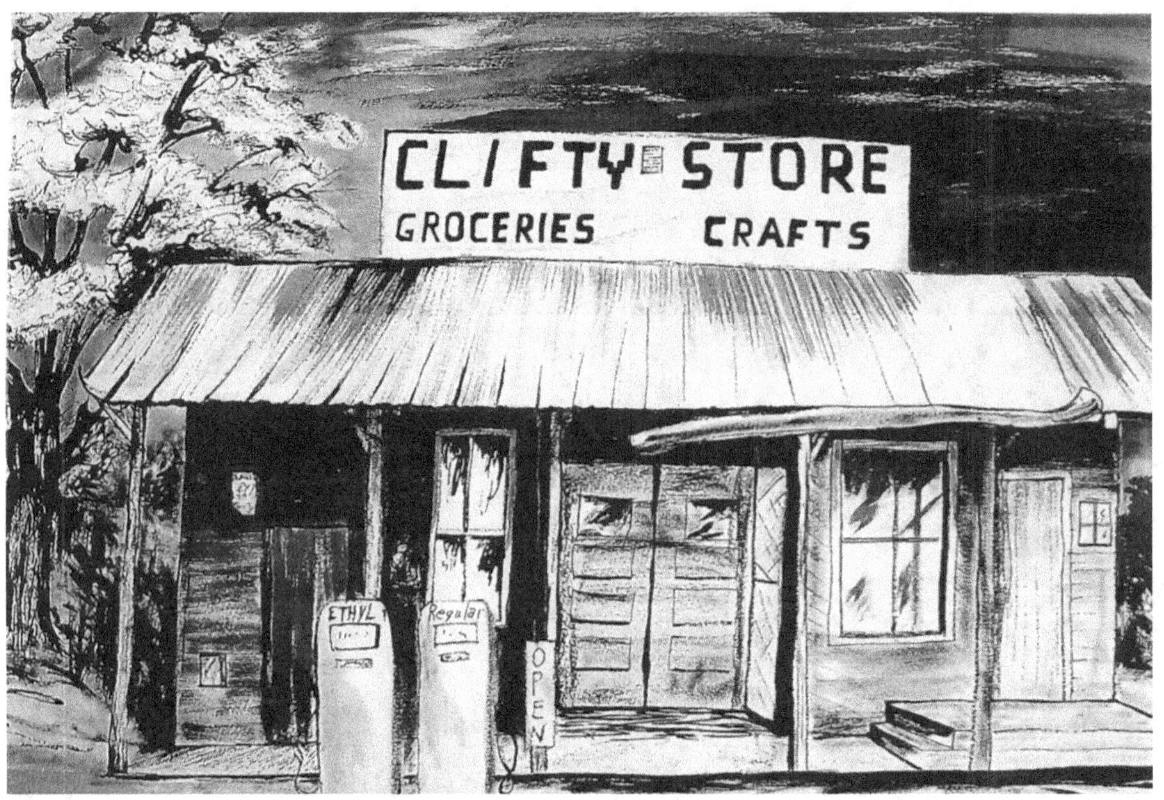

Illustration 101: *Clifty Store*

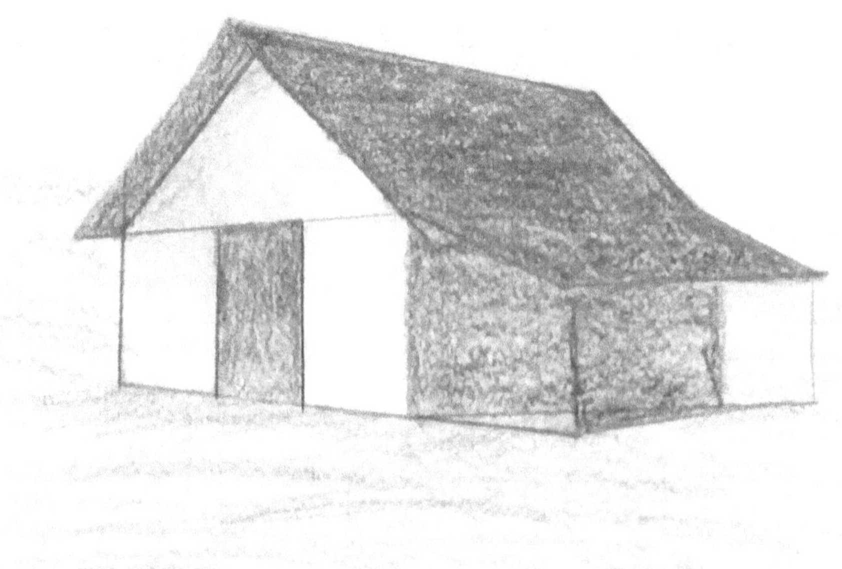

Illustration 102: another old building

ANIMALS

There are any number of animals you may start drawing with a rectangle. Study what you decide to draw before starting. Think of it in
shapes you are familiar with, and begin to lightly draw those shapes.
Give the shape form by shading, and before you know it, you are
drawing with ease. You need to study what you are going to draw
(did I say that once?). It is important. Investigation is about two-thirds
of getting the drawing right.

If you are not sure of the angle of the line, see Illustration 103 below. Get the angle right by the clock. Hold a pencil at arm's length,
with one eye closed. Line the pencil up with the line you are drawing.
Without moving the pencil, open your eyes and look at the pencil,
then at the hour hand on the clock. What time is the pencil pointing
to? Draw a line the same angle as the pencil.

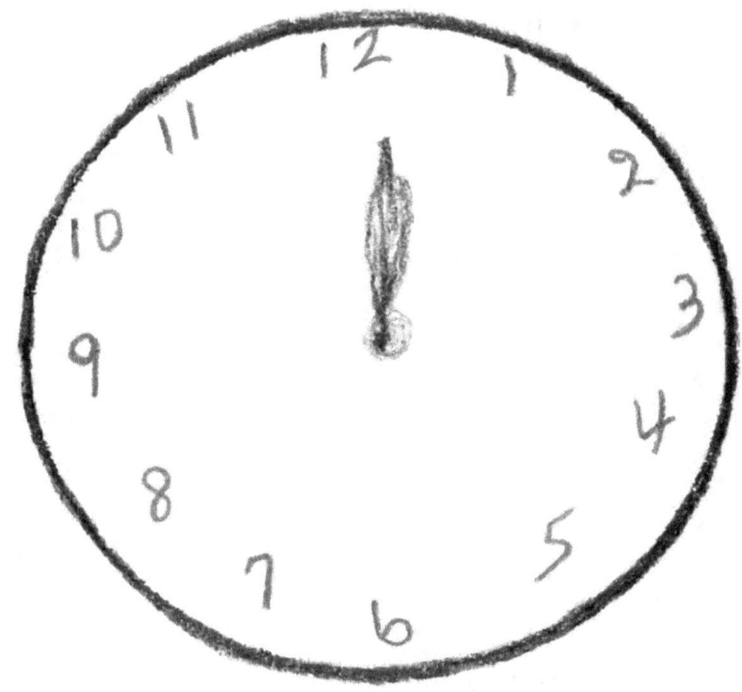

Illustration 103

Bobcat

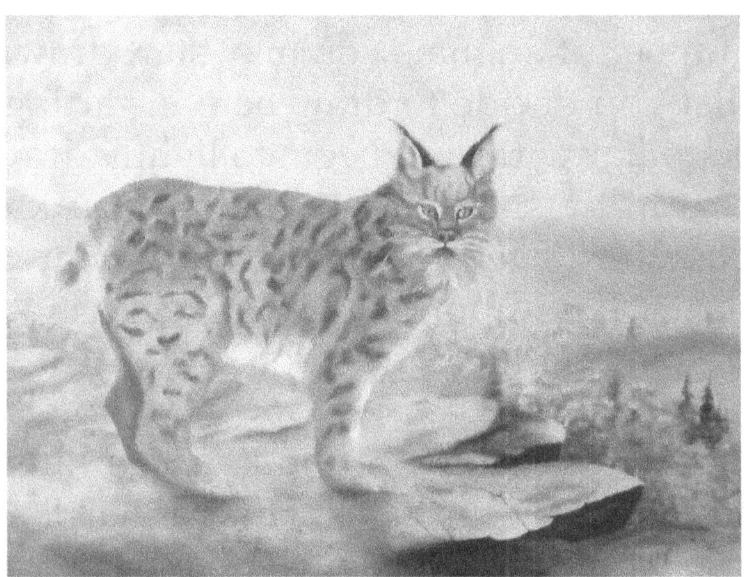

Illustration 104: *The Bobcat Is Watching*, oil

Look at the print of the bobcat, and draw a light rectangle for his body. Remember, it will be easier if you look ahead at all the drawings for the bobcat before starting.

Illustration 105

The rectangle is tilted a little higher on the left. The angle of top line would be about 9:10 on the face of a clock (see illustration 103).

Notice how his back goes in and out of the rectangle. His tail starts where the back touches the top left of the rectangle, and the rump comes out a little below that. Draw a circle for his head.

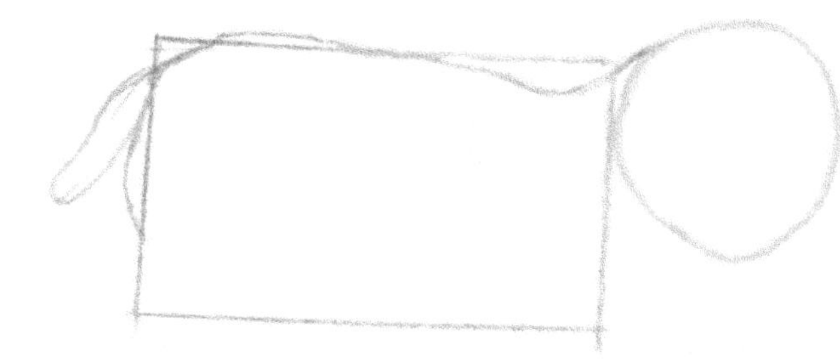

Illustration 106

Draw teardrops for his ears, and one for his rump and hind leg. You will finish his face using an enlarged face later. We are beginning to bring the drawing together.

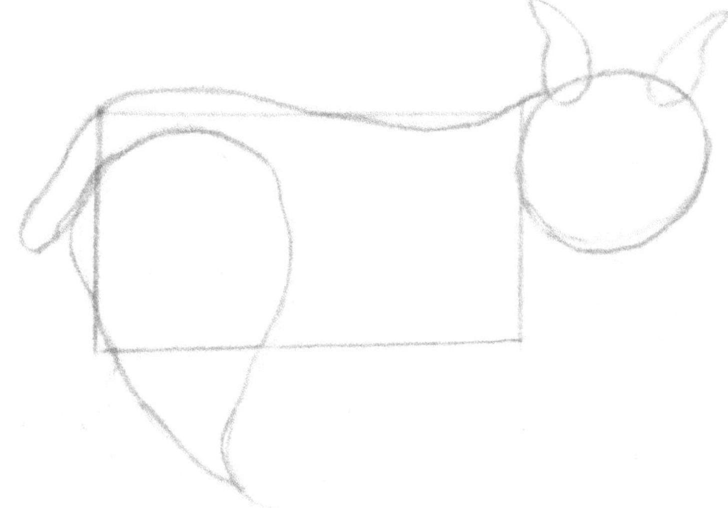

Illustration 107

Notice how the back legs are shaped and where they fit together with the rest of the body. His hind leg comes into view just before his right leg goes back into the rectangle. The light tummy starts going down outside the bottom line. Draw the legs and chest the same way by following the illustration carefully.

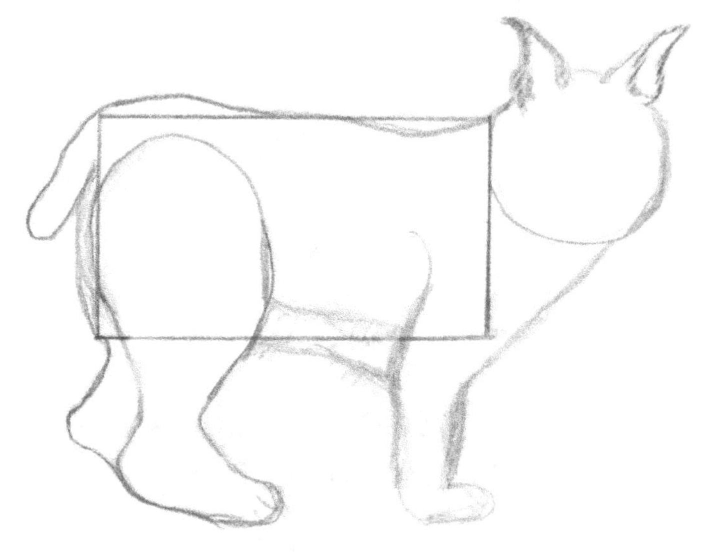

Illustration 108

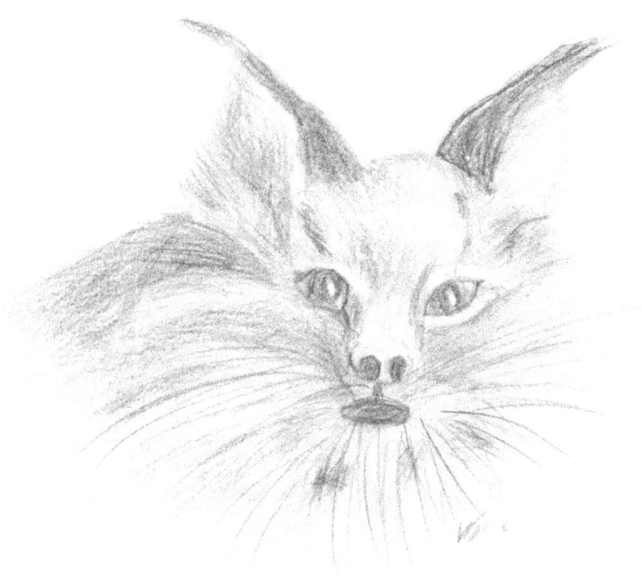

Illustration 109

The head is the last thing to draw. It is enlarged in Illustration 109 to show the details more clearly.

The eyes have a dark outline around them and down each side of the nose. Put the highlight on the end of the nose.

It has hair all over, so there is no actual outline drawing of the face, except the light circle you drew at first. Remember to draw its whiskers last. The line centered beneath the nose joins a triangle forming the top lip. Draw that triangle.

See the highlights in the eyes. The highlights can be seen in both eyes from the same light source. Therefore, if the light hits the left eye in the upper left, it will also hit the right eye in the upper left. Highlights are one of the most important things about living images.

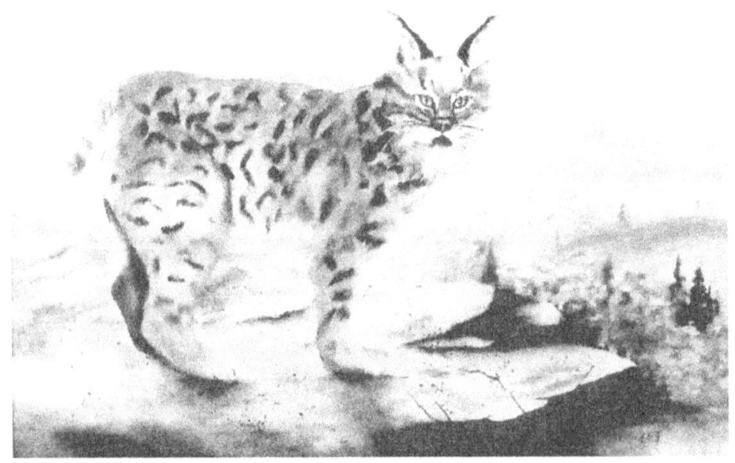

Illustration 110

You may wish to color it with colored pencils or shade it with varying shades of black. You have just drawn a bobcat. Great job!

Red Fox

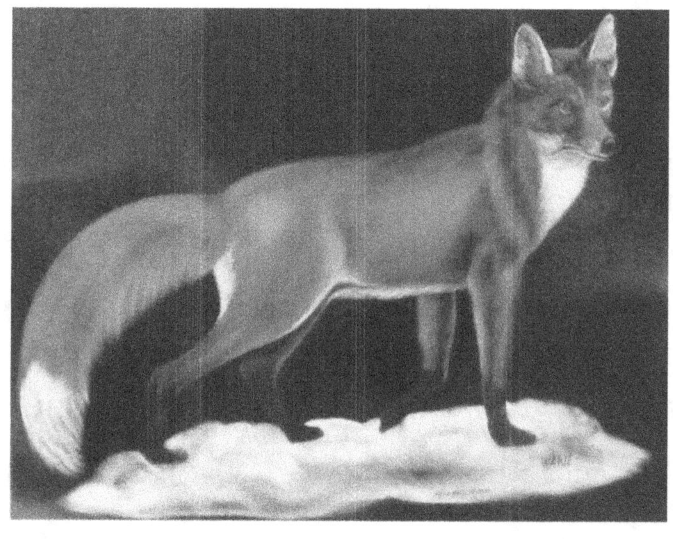

The red fox is a beautiful creature. This was done with soft pastels on black pastel paper.

Illustration 111

I saw my first red fox in the wild when I was only six or eight years of age. I stood frozen in my tracks, and so did he. My first thought was "that is the most beautiful creature I have ever seen."

That was one of my most memorable moments. It was many years later when I painted it from memory. I learned to visualize before I knew what it meant.

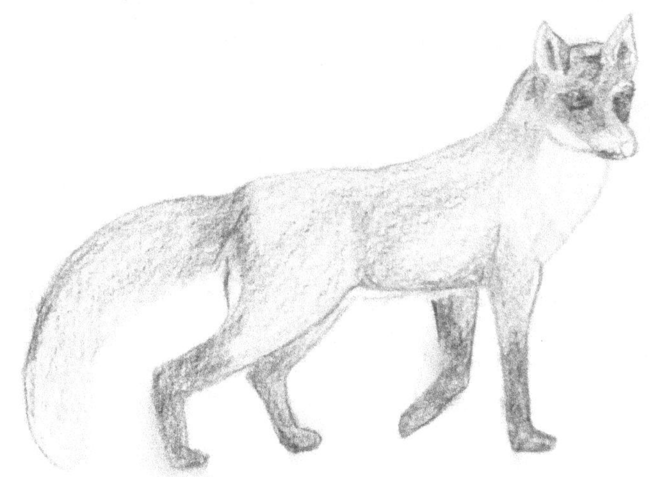

Do you see the graceful lines? Do you see any rectangles? Any teardrops? Can you see the tilted neck and the tilted rectangular body and the teardrops for the head and neck? Can you see the teardrop hind leg and the ears? Let's draw it.

Illustration 112

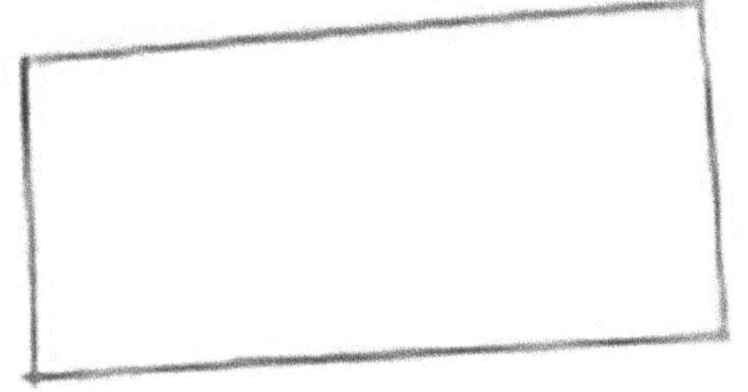

Draw a tilted rectangle for the body. Tilt it at about 2:30. See Illustration 103 for the clock face.

Illustration 113

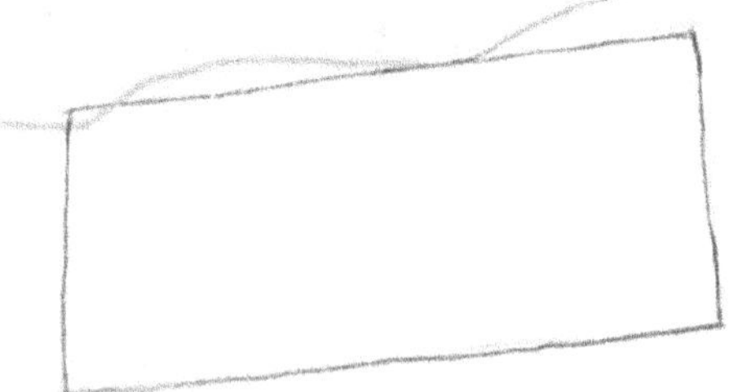

Draw the neck above the rectangle, come down to the top line, and go along the line. Curve the back up over the line again. Come back inside the rectangle, then outside the rectangle, and begin the tail.

Illustration 114

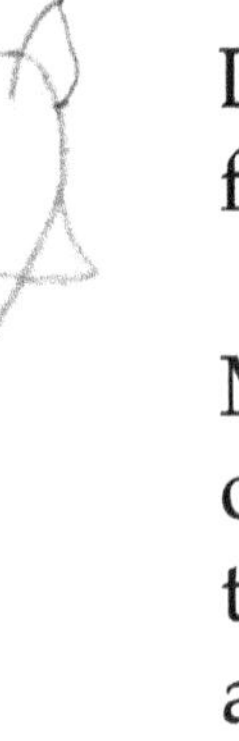

Draw a teardrop for his head and one for each ear. Make one for his neck.

Make the teardrop for his hip and part of his hind leg. Pay special attention to this teardrop. It will need to be drawn at just the right angle. See where the hip comes into the rectangle and where it comes out. It is angled back.

Illustration 115

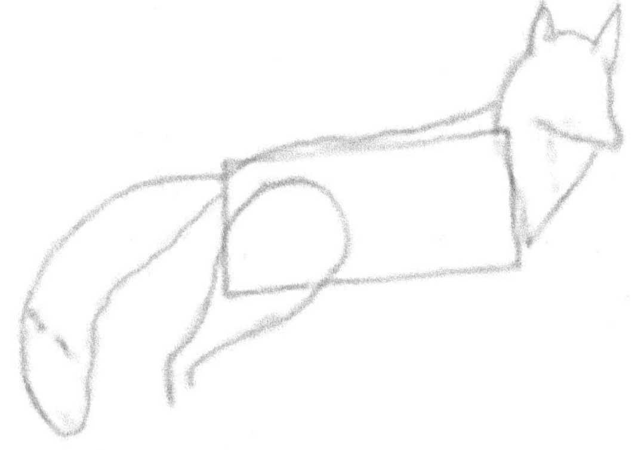

Draw the tail. I have put some scribbles where the white will be.

Illustration 116

Draw the feet and legs. It won't
be difficult if you study this illustration closely for where to
come out of the body and how
far down to come.

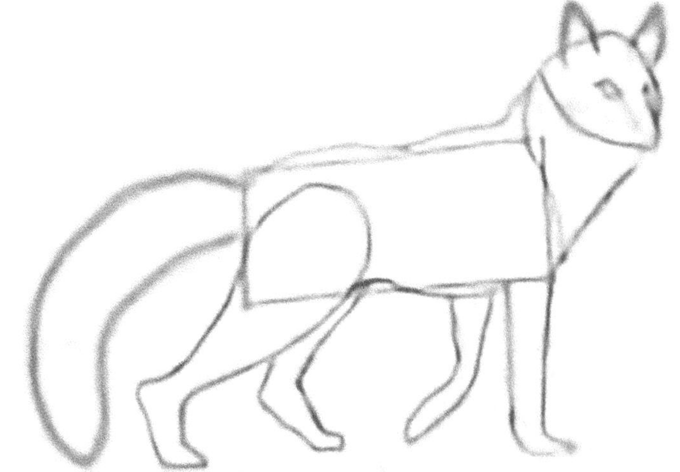

Illustration 117

I have enlarged his face for
you. Start shading his eyes
first. Remember the light
comes into both eyes from the
same direction.

See the dark down both sides
of the nose. Blacken the tip of
his nose, but leave the highlight on the top of his nose.

Darken the insides of both
ears, but leave the outsides of
the ears light. The lower side
of his face and upper part of
his neck under his chin should
be white.

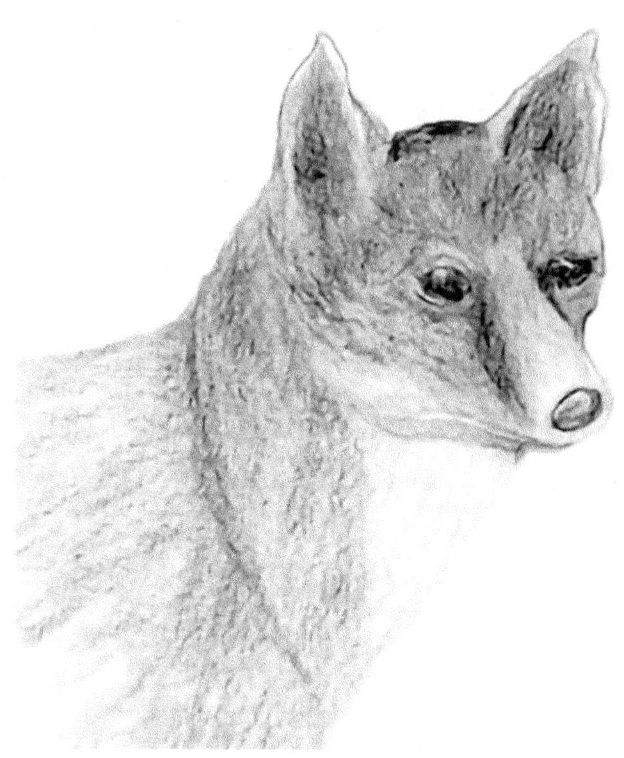

Illustration 118

His feet and legs are black over halfway up, and there is black around
his eyes. The end of the tail is white. Part of his cheek and the front
of his throat are white. His tummy and under his tail and down the
backs of his hind legs are also white.

HORSES

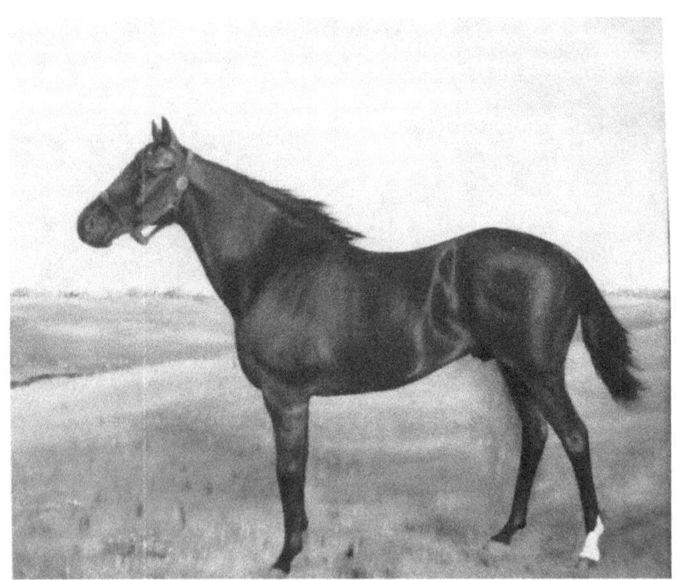

Illustration 119: *The Thoroughbred*, oil

Would you like to draw a horse? They aren't as complicated as they look. If possible, study a few horses. Learn more about the different breeds from books or magazines. You will want to draw them in action, but need to know how they look and move.

Thoroughbred

We will start with a thoroughbred, which can run longer races than some other breeds. It usually has a long slim body and longer legs.

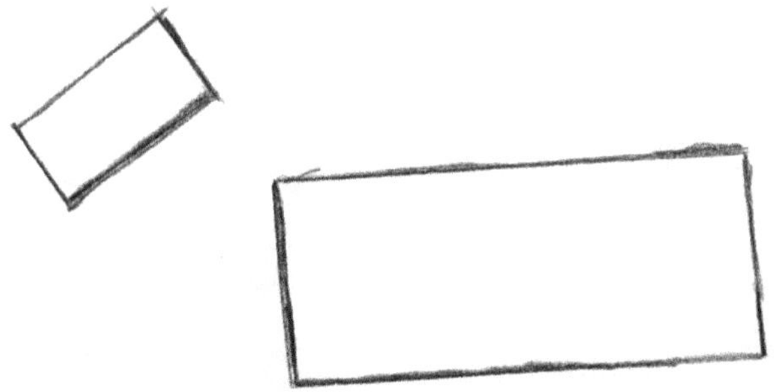

Illustration 120

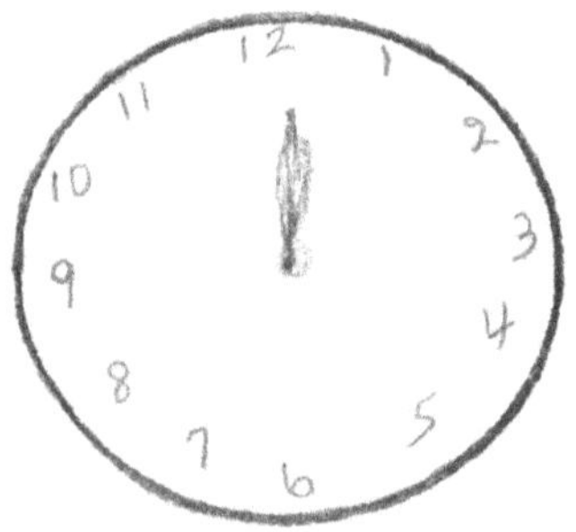

Illustration 121

Both rectangles are tilted, as they should be. The clock face is repeated here for reference. The angle of the rectangle for the head is at about 2:00, and the other rectangle is at about 2:45.

Draw a teardrop for his rump to the back of the knee. Observe the placement within the rectangle.

Draw the outline for the head inside the small rectangle. Then draw tear-drops for the ears. The face will be drawn last. Draw the bottom of the neck slanted down from the cheek-bone. It has a curved-out place just before it comes into the bottom left corner of the bottom rectangle. See where the top of the neck comes out from behind the ear. The neck joins the body about one third of the way up on the large rectangle.

The back curves below the line and comes back out. Notice how the rump and the curved-in part of the back leg comes together. See how the stomach curves inside the bottom line.

Draw the legs, being careful where to curve them. The legs on the far side don't go down as far as the ones nearest you. Why? Because they are further away.

Illustration 124 is the outline, except for the face.

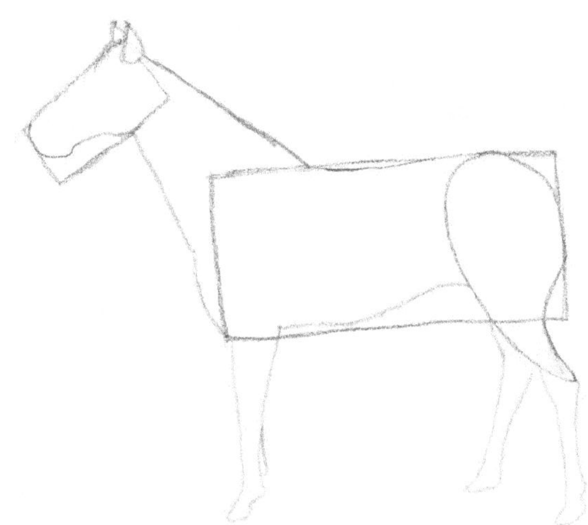

Illustration 122

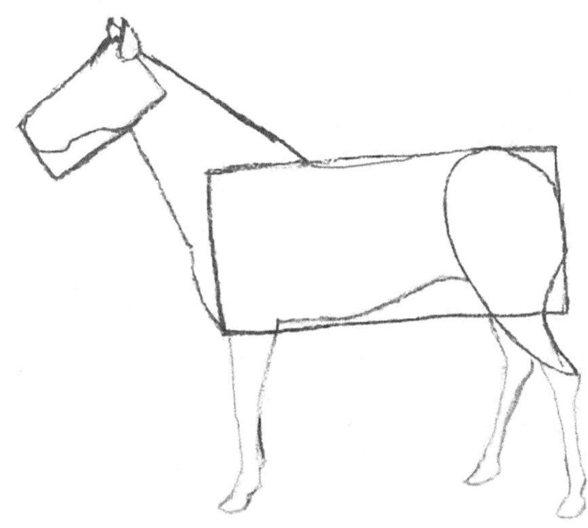

Illustration 123

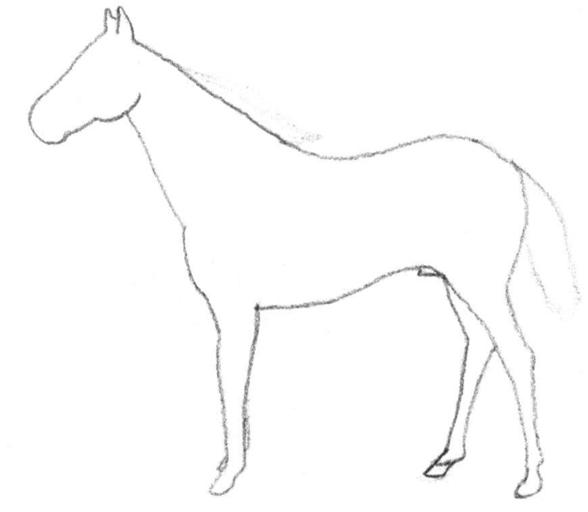

Illustration 124

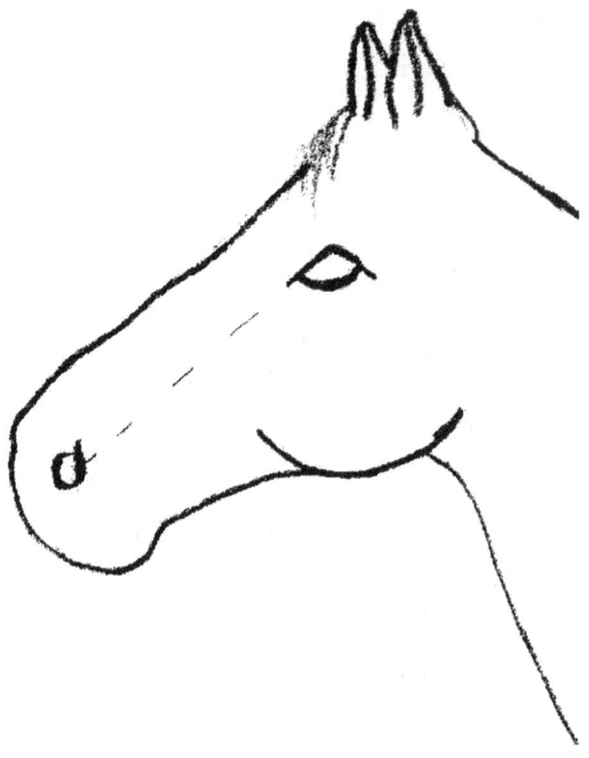

Illustration 125

This is how the outline of the head should look. Notice the nose goes in a line parallel with the front of the face. The parallel starts from the front of the eye. The eye is made like a triangle with a curved bottom. You can see how the head is finished.

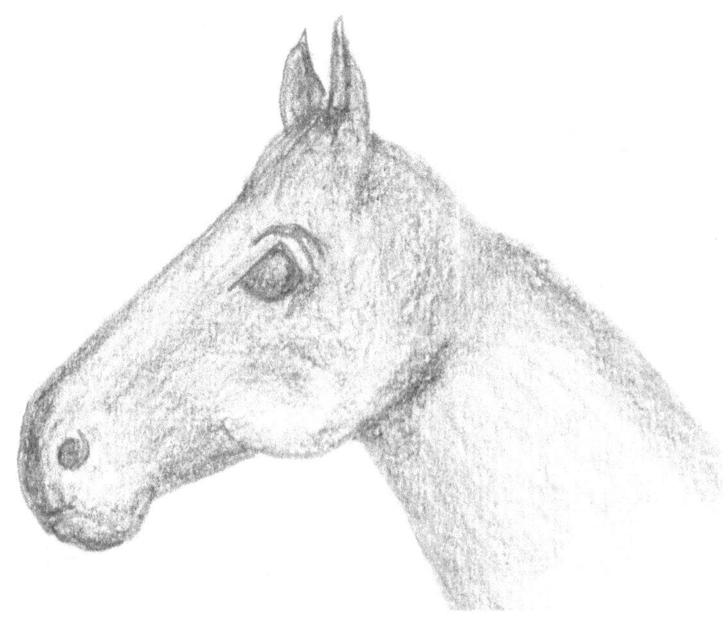

Illustration 126

Quarter Horse

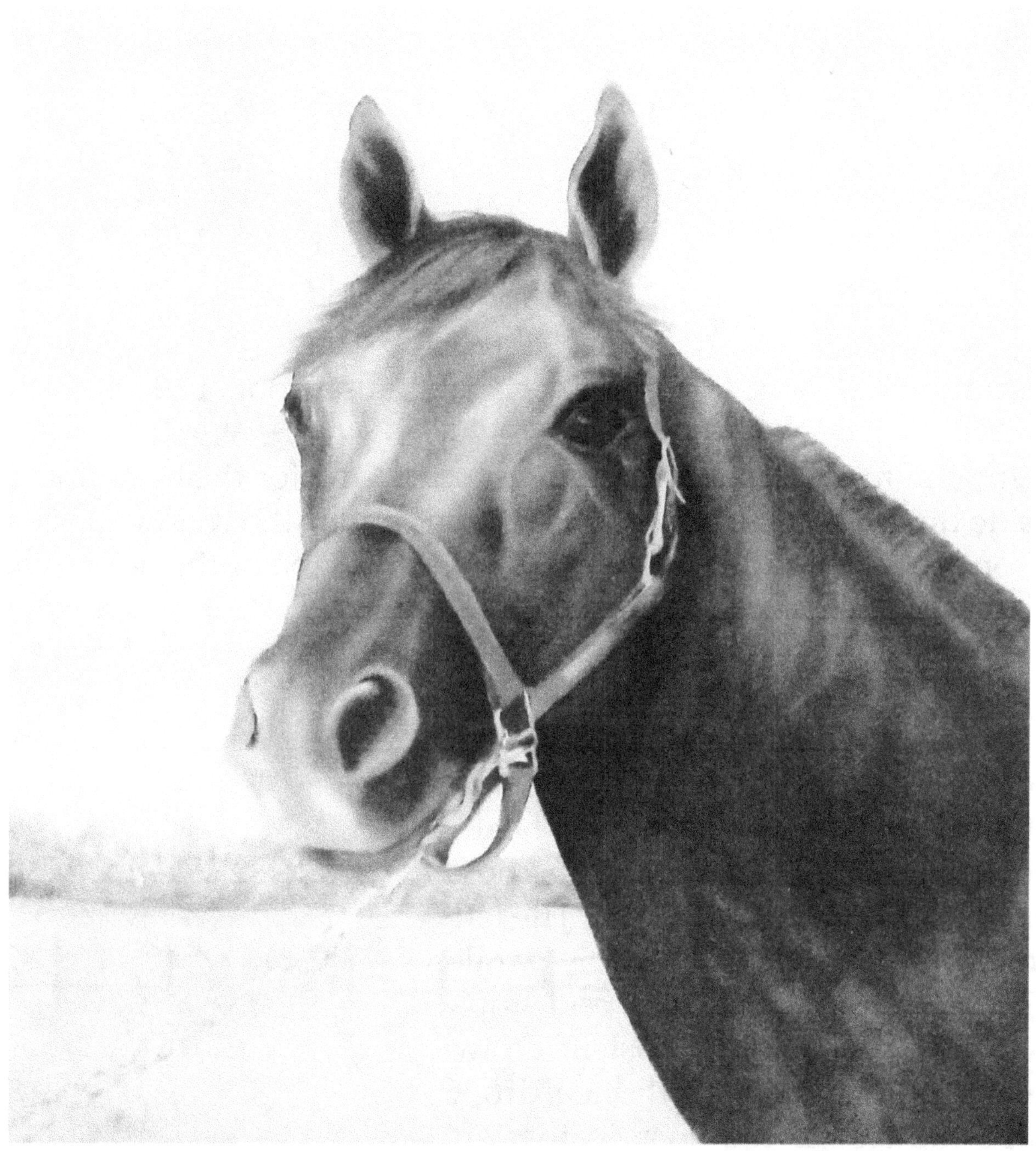

Illustration 127: *Sire of Champions*, oil

This is a Quarter Horse, which is a breed of horse that specializes in a quarter-mile race.

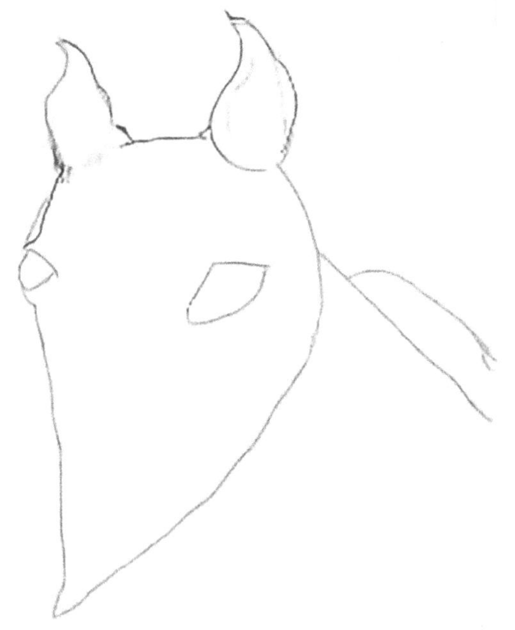

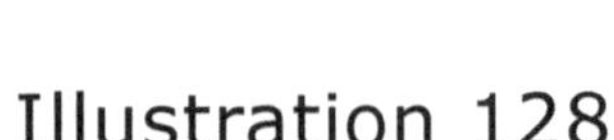
Illustration 128

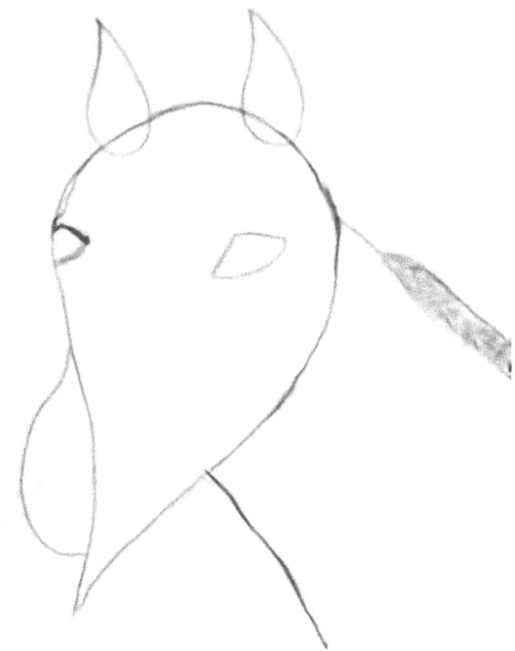
Illustration 129

Begin with four teardrops: two for the ears, one for the head and one upside down at the bottom left (see Illustration 129). Can you see the reason for that fourth teardrop? It is for the shape of the nose, which is a bit different from that of the thoroughbred.

The left eye goes down and against the left side of the teardrop for his head. The right eye (a triangle with the bottom curved) is beneath the ear. The left side of the eye points down, is parallel with the front of the face, and stops at the top of the right nostril. Draw the right jawline inside the teardrop. Shape the rest of the nose in the left bottom teardrop.

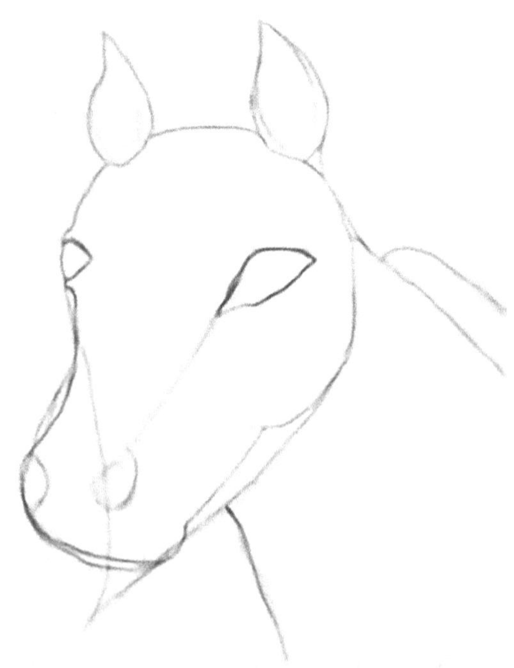
Illustration 130

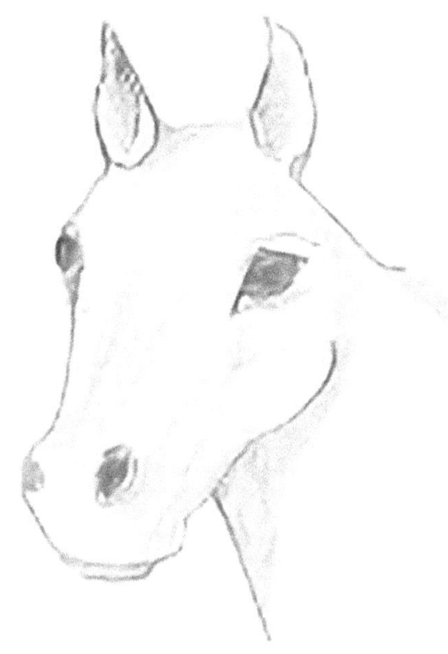

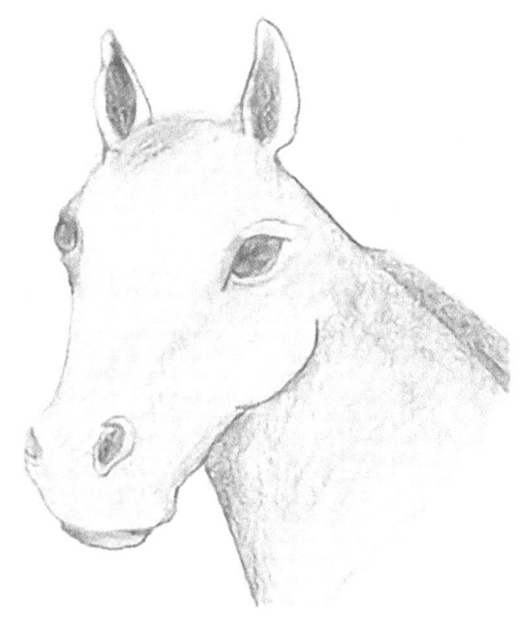

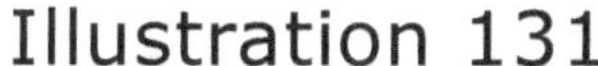
Illustration 131   Illustration 132

Illustration 131 shows the beginning of the shading. The finished drawing and shading are shown in Illustration 132.

Notice that there is no highlight in the horse's eye. You can't put a highlight without making the horse look scared or mad. Put just a small smudge of a lighter color in his eye. You are doing great!

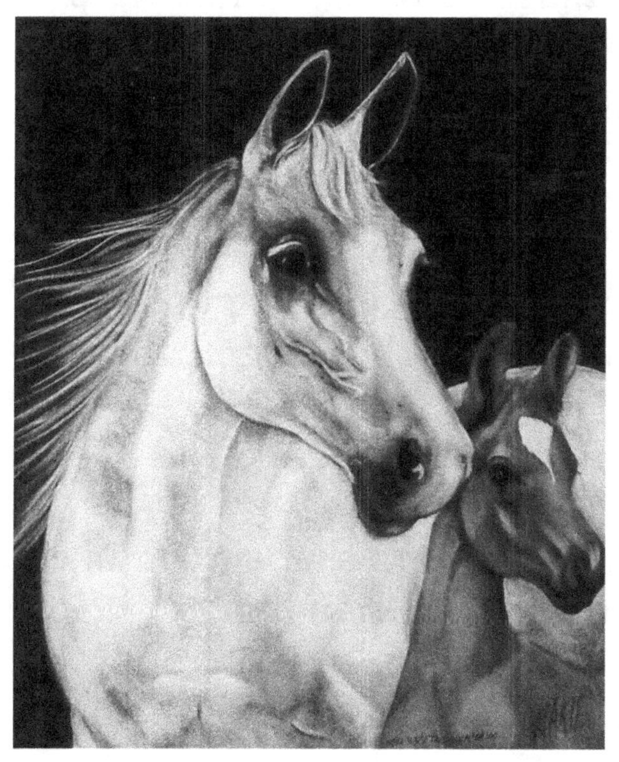

Every breed of horse is capable of turning his ears all the way forward, or each ear to the outside, or all the way back. The ears are facing front if they are listening intently, or turned all the way back when they are angry or running races.

This is an Arabian mare and her foal.

Illustration 133: *Mare and Colt*, soft pastels on black pastel paper

PEOPLE

If you want to put incidental people in your art, but not as a principal part of the work, a simple way to do this is by drawing stick people.

Develop it with each step. You do not need detail, but you need to know how to add more detail when needed.

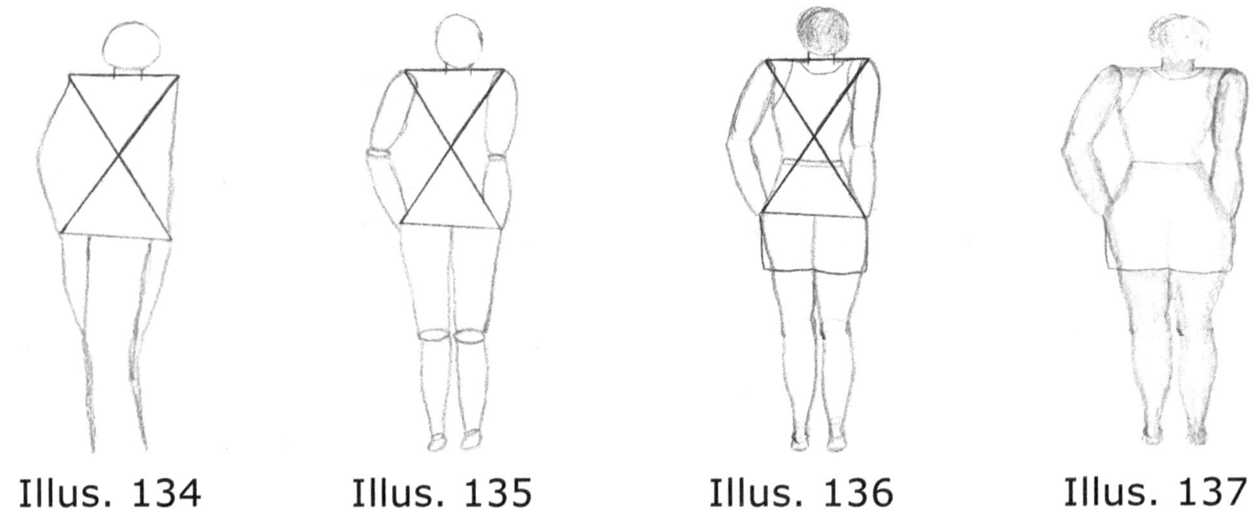

Illus. 134   Illus. 135   Illus. 136   Illus. 137

Illustration 134: Start with two triangles. Use these as a guide for the width of the shoulders and hips. The two triangles will work for a man or woman.

The place where the upside-down triangle and the right-side-up triangle meet marks where the waist will be, not how big it will be.

Illustration 135: Draw arms and legs to look like a manikin.

Illustration 136: Erase the manikin-like joints and shape them like a man's limbs. Draw his body, and put some clothes on him.

Illustration 137: Erase the two triangles. Add the rest of the shading.

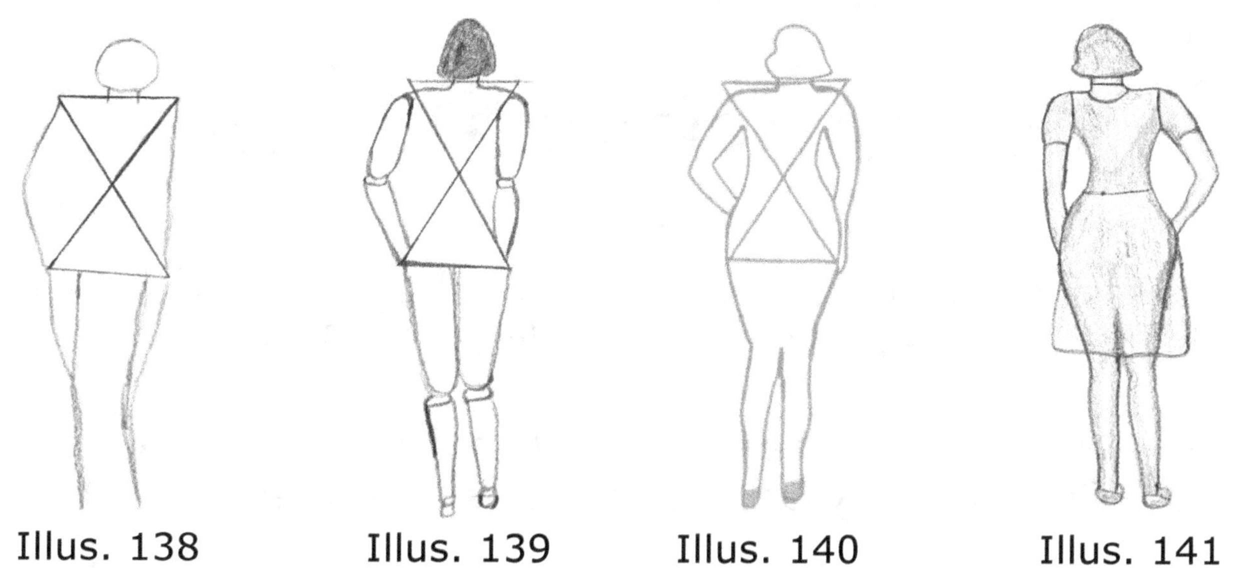

Illus. 138   Illus. 139   Illus. 140   Illus. 141

Illustration 138: Start with a stick person for the woman also. Her shoulders will be dropped some for, by nature, she has a smaller frame.

Illustration 139: Shape up her arms and legs, making them look like a manikin's joints.

Illustration 140: Make the manikin-like joints more like a real woman's arms and legs.

Illustration 141: Put clothes on her, and shade her. You want to erase the two triangles.

This is just a thought on how to make people a part of your art without much effort.

See how easy it was to draw people from behind? Practice this, and you will learn how to draw faces later. It will be easier than you think.

You will be able to leave out some steps on the things I am teaching. The steps are just to speed up the learning process.

PORTRAITS

Portraits are a different story. The person the portrait is of (the one paying for it) wants it to be lifelike, realistic, and flattering.

When I am drawing a portrait, I try to capture the attitude of the person. This is done by facial expression and posture.

We are not drawing faces in this book. However, here are some tips on drawing portraits and some things to think about, as well as questions to ask.

Examples of types of portraits are busts or full body. It is important to get a likeness in either case.

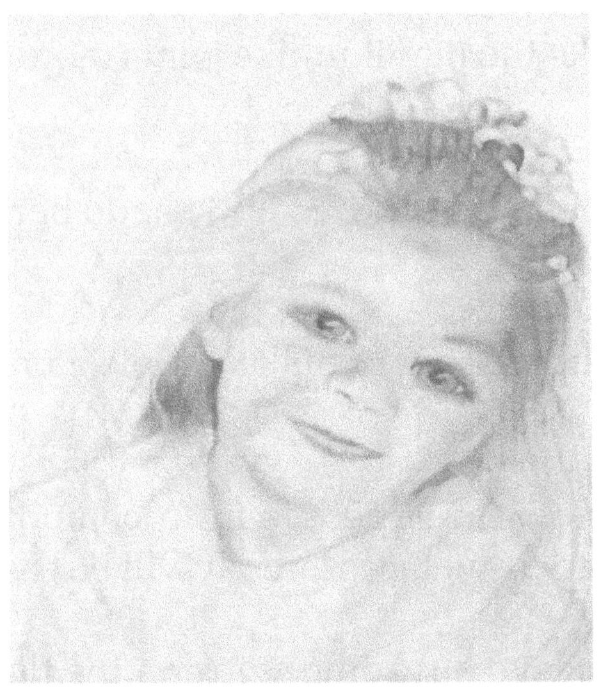

Illustration 142: pencil

Note the sparkle in the eyes. Whether you are drawing a portrait or not, you need to make it convincing.

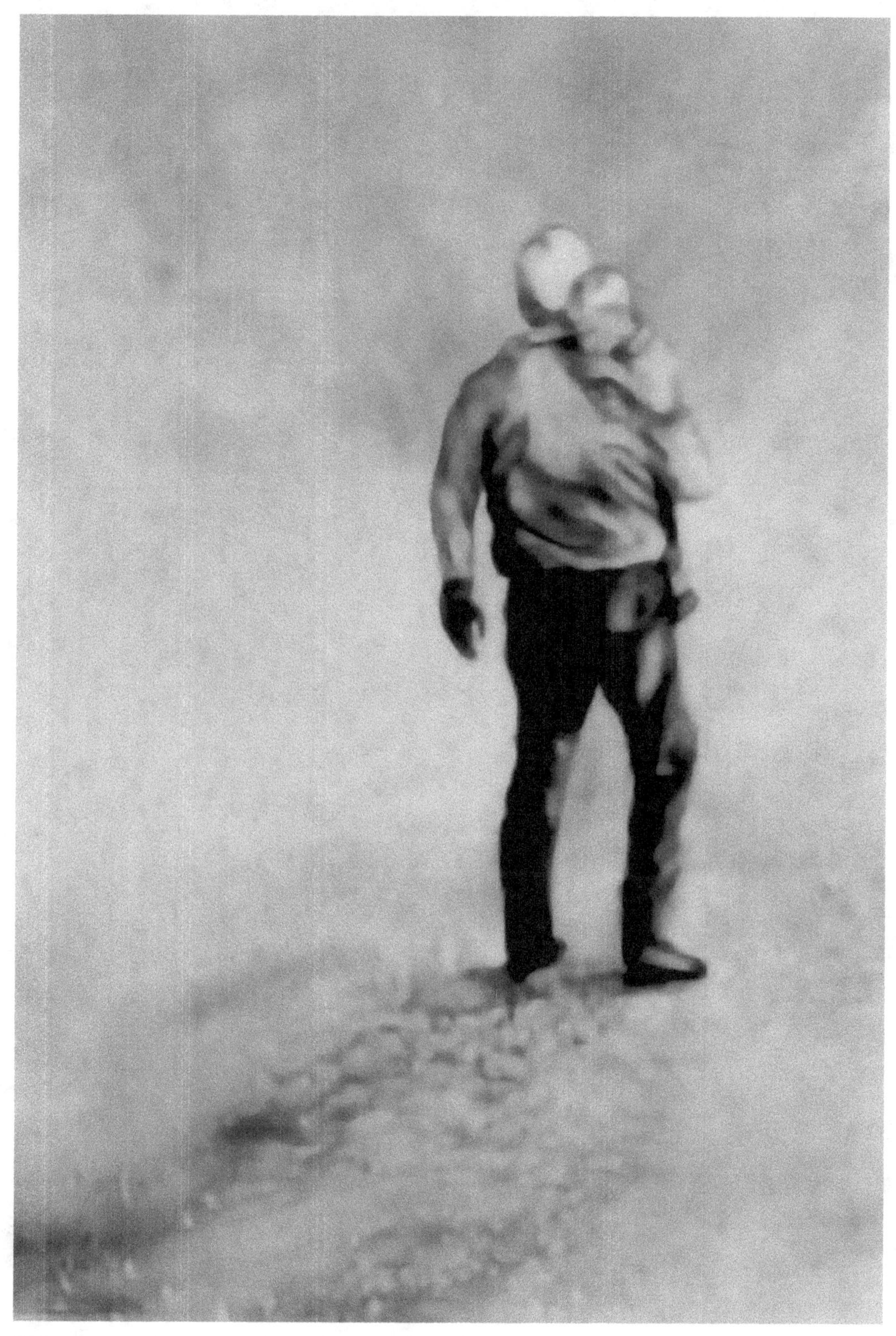

Illustration 143: *Grandpa's Boy*, watercolor

Grandpa carrying his grandson out of harm's way. Did I capture the meaning?

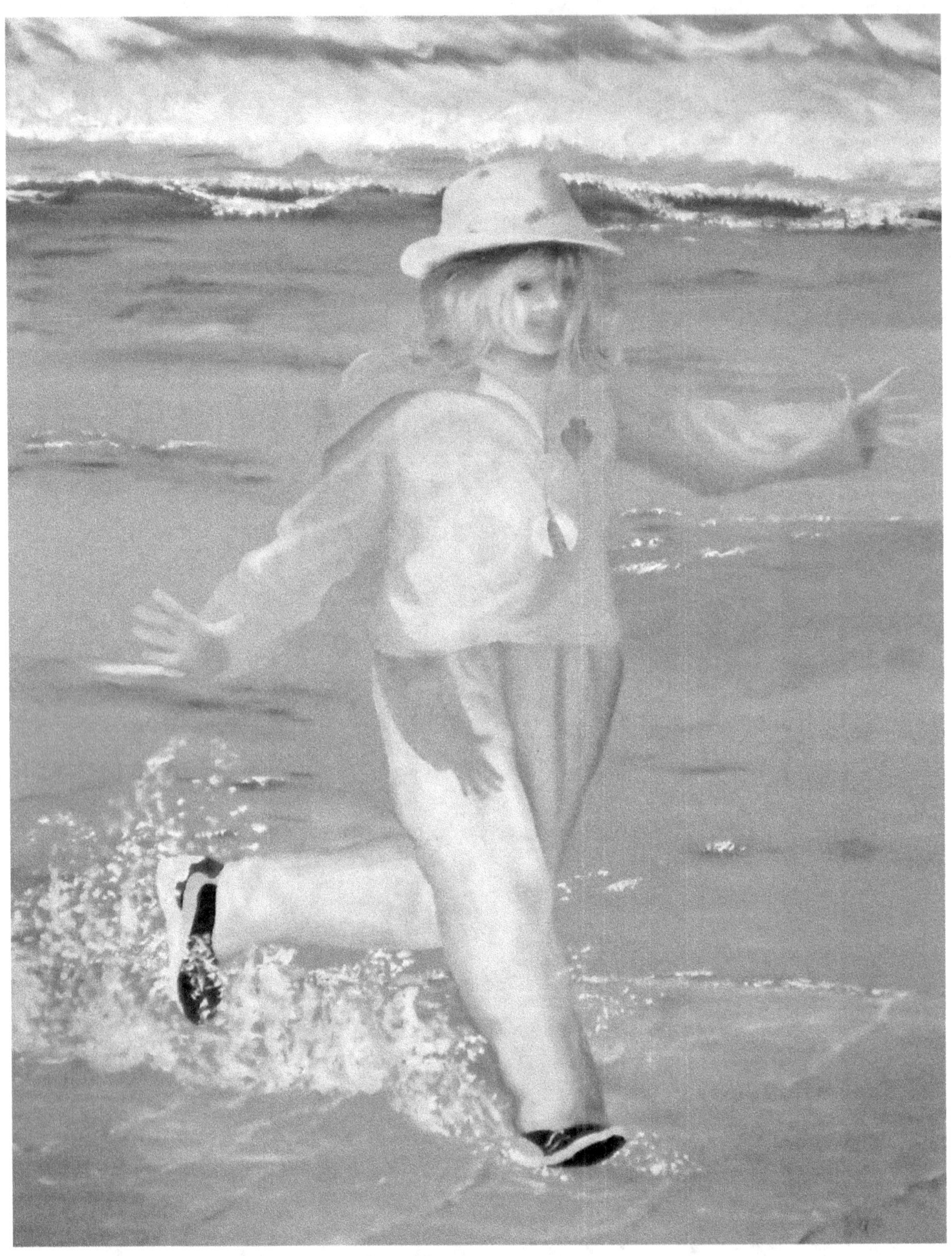

Illustration 144: *Wild Child*, oil

A grandchild is playing with the ocean waves.

Let your art tell a story or create an emotion.

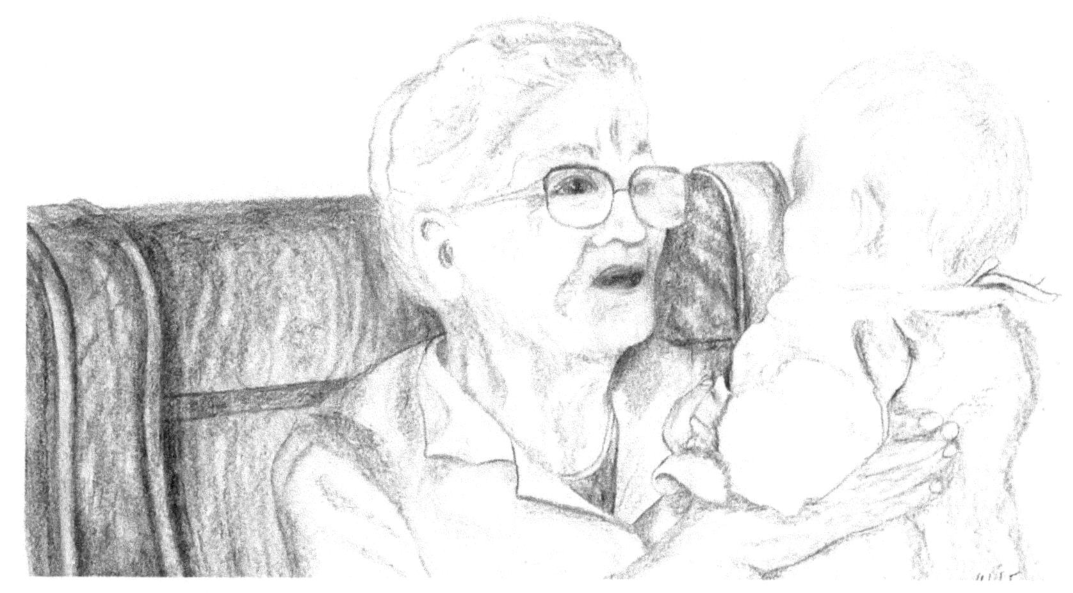

Illustration 145

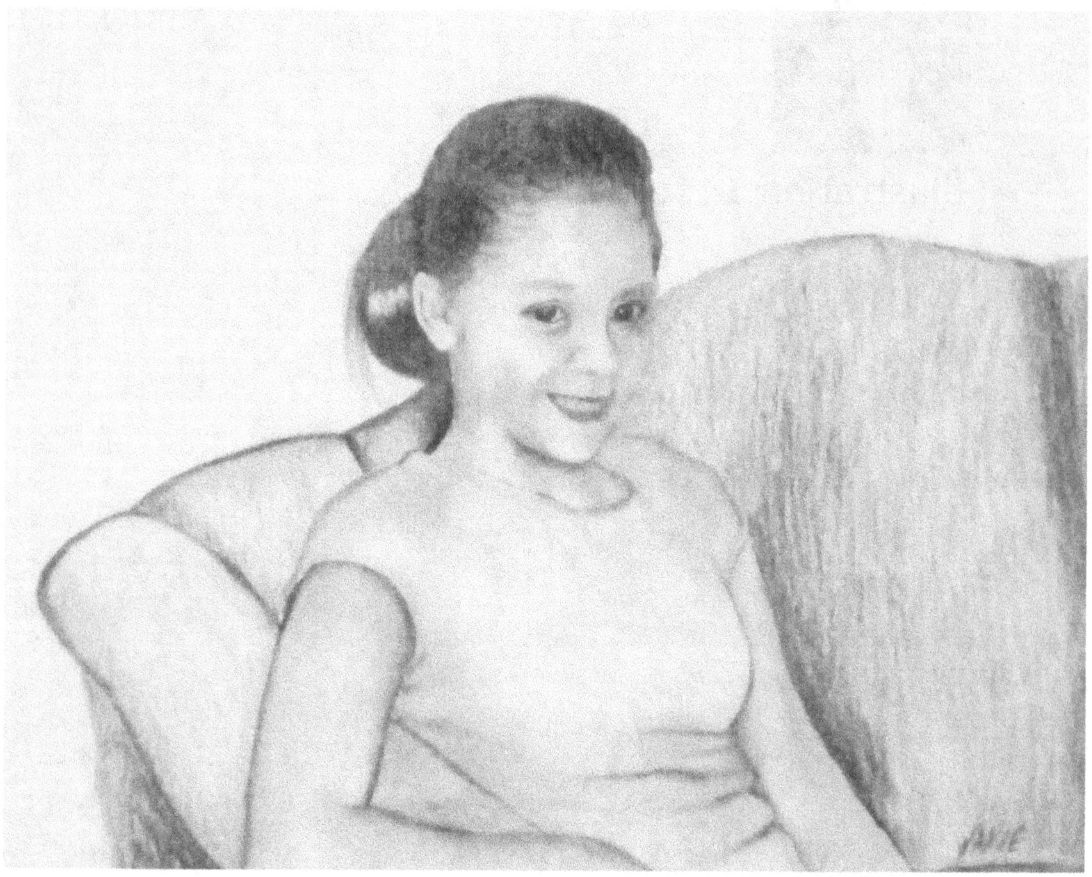

Illustration 146

Does the person look natural? Can you see the sparkle in the eyes? Does her posture look relaxed? These are good questions to ask.

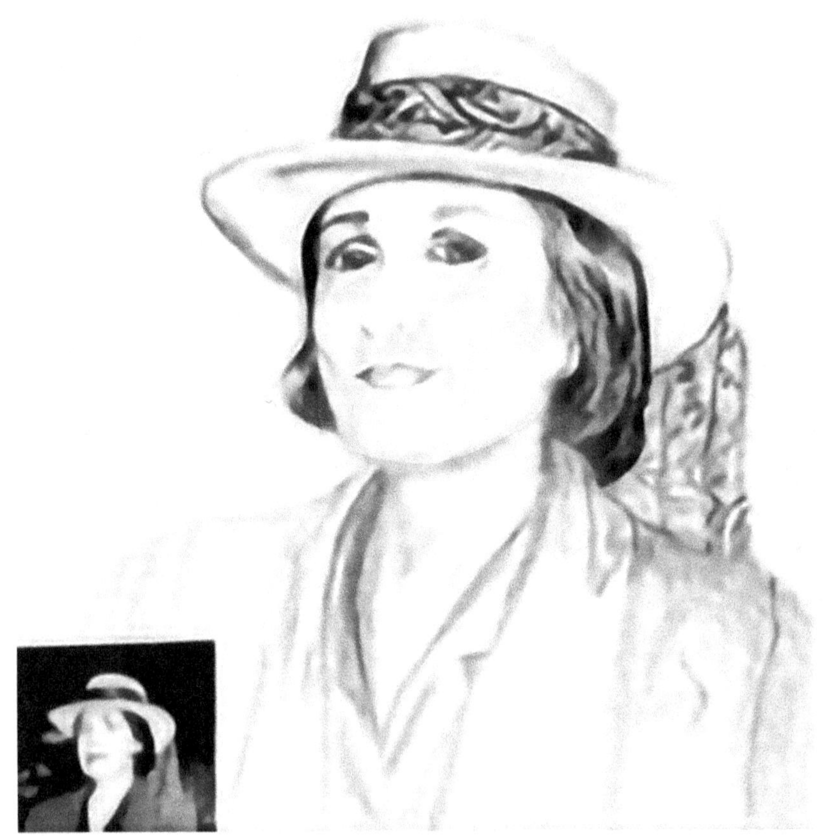

Illustration 147: *A Classy Lady*

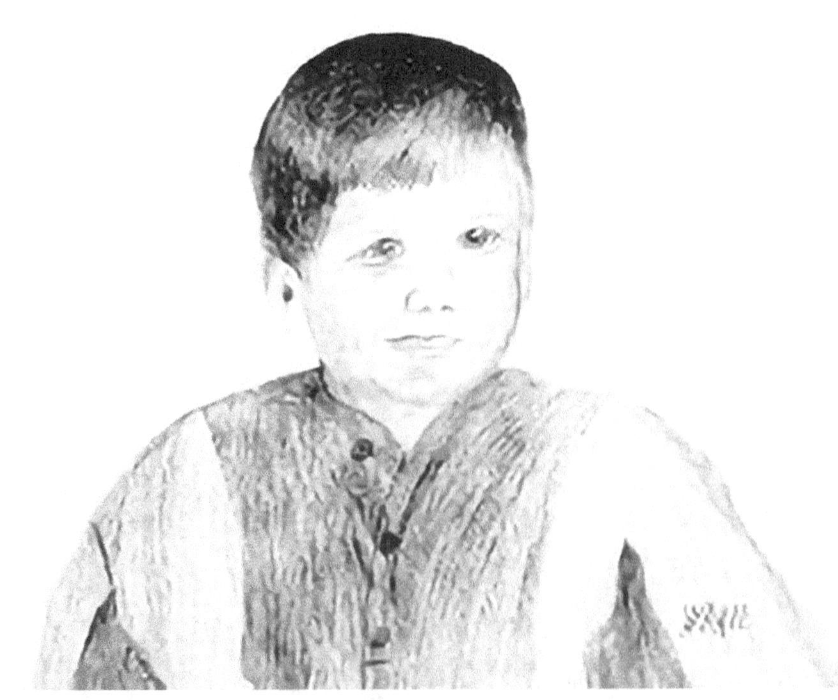

Illustration 148: *Just Being a Boy*

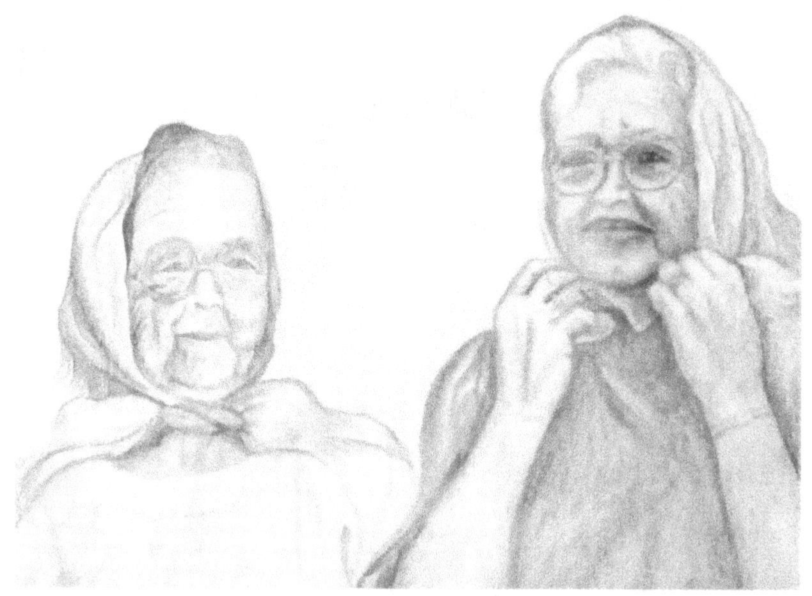

Illustration 149: *Old Friends*

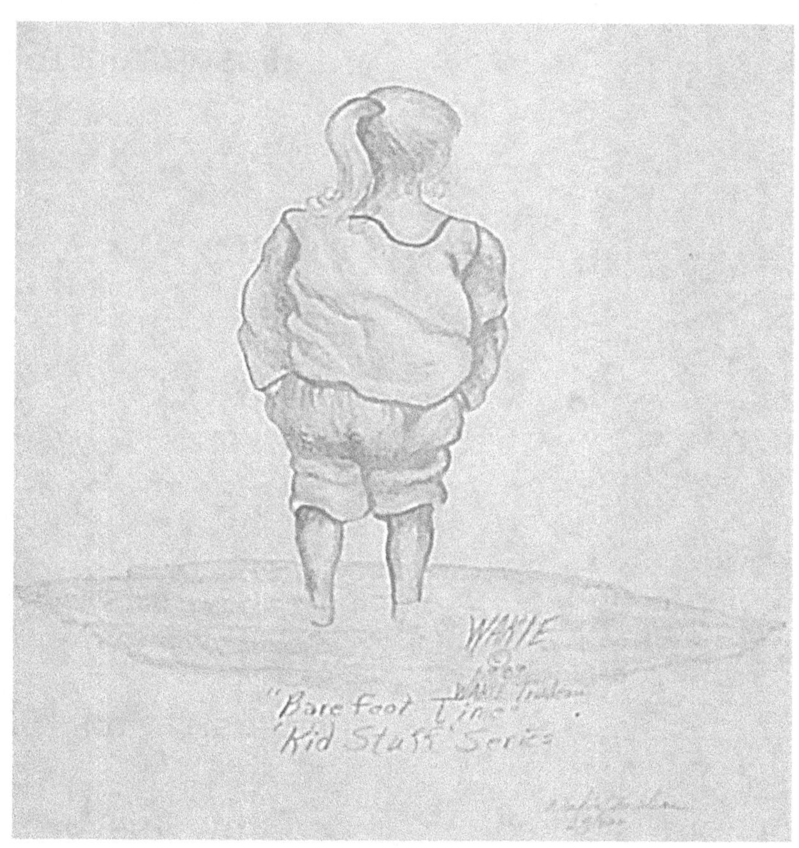

Illustration 150: *Barefoot Time*

This is one of a series I did before I drew people's faces.

SANTA

Let's have some fun drawing Santa.

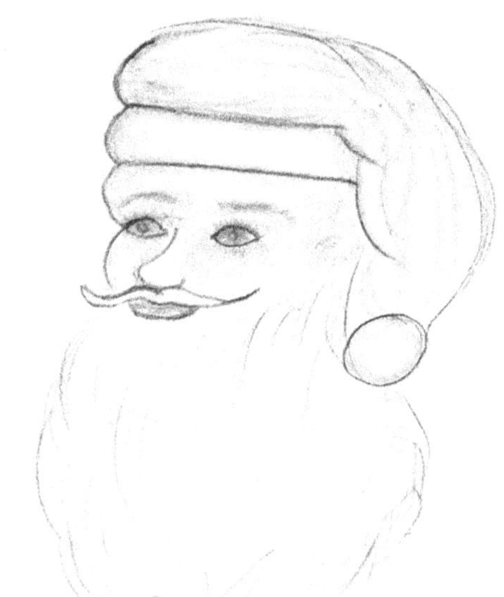

Illustration 151

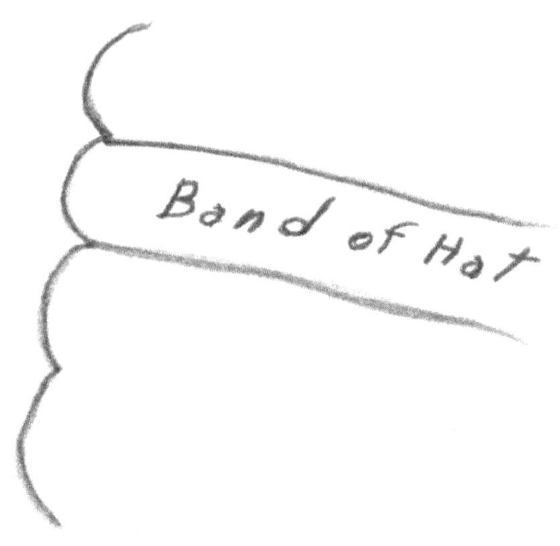

Illustration 152

He starts with four stacked parentheses. Draw two slant-ed lines (about 9:30), which become part of his hat.

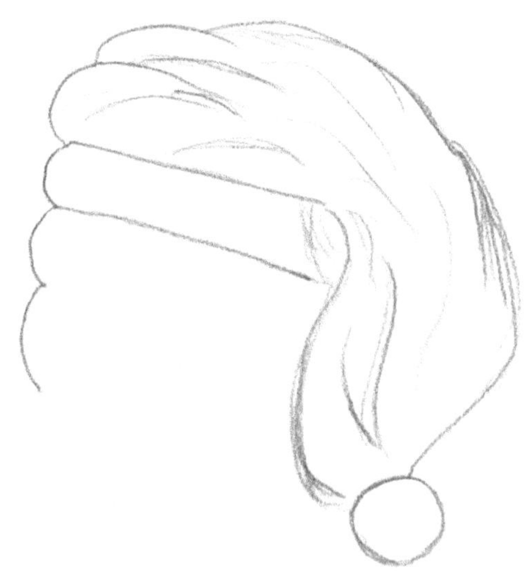

Illustration 153

Draw his hat by using the top two parentheses. Make a round ball on the end.

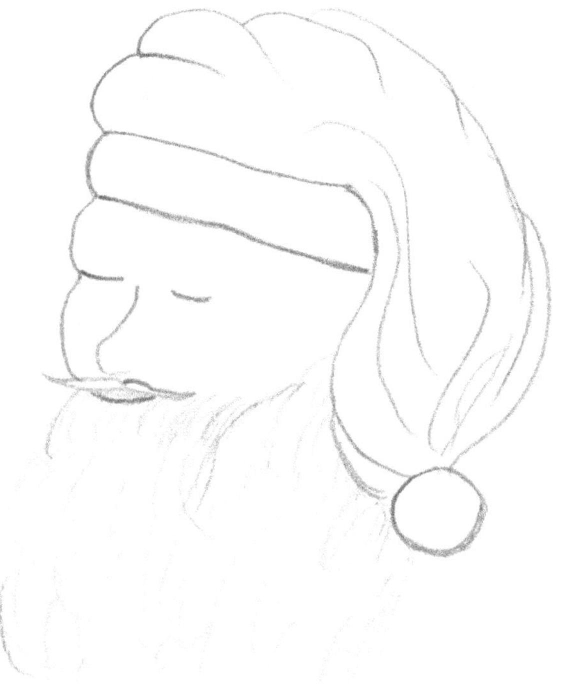

Draw the eyes closed first. You will use them later for the bottom of the eyes. Draw a question mark upside down and backward for a nose.

His mustache is centered under his nose. Draw the bottom lip and start his beard.

Illustration 154

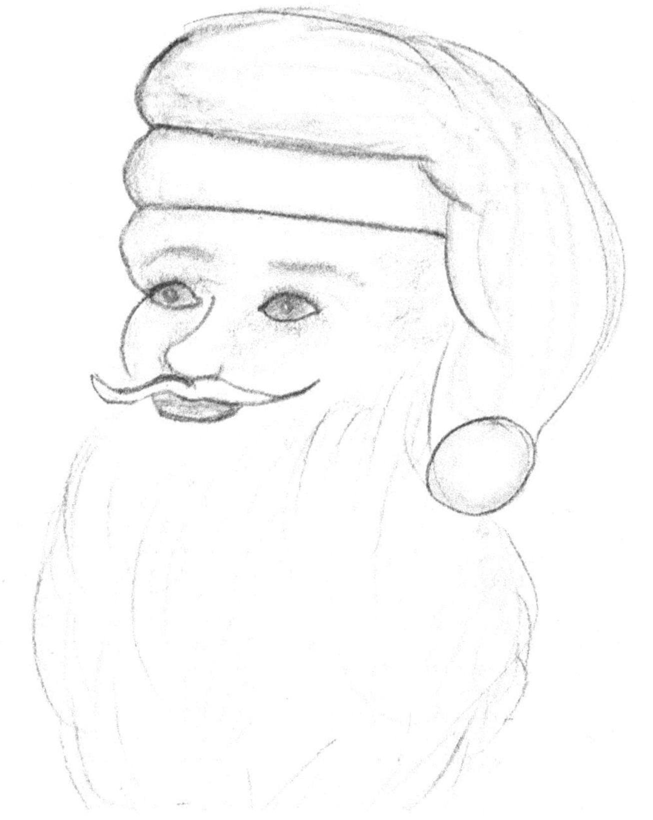

Draw the top of his eyes, eyebrows, and eyelashes. Shade him. Notice, I only shaded left and right ends of the band of his cap and the outside edge of the ball of his cap. They are left white.

Illustration 155

SUMMATION

It takes practice to become a good artist. You never stop learning. Now that you have a good base for drawing, shading, and applying perspective, you will learn quickly as you observe and draw more. It may be drawing the back of a head, a tree, or a pet. Everything is a subject.

If you carry a sketch pad and pencil or pen with you and learn to put on paper what you see before you, it will become a valuable tool.

Everyone becomes a critic, even your mother, your best friend, or a stranger. Don't let them bother you. You can learn a lot from them just by listening to them and weighing it out. If you don't agree with them, cast it aside. If you do agree, you have learned an important lesson. You may respond to them, "Can you show me how? I'm always trying to learn." Try not to take criticism personally. You are not in competition with anyone.

I hope you enjoyed this book as much as I enjoyed drawing the illustrations and gathering the information from years of learning and teaching.

Thank you for allowing me the privilege of sharing with you my love of art.

Enjoy drawing!

About the Author

Wakie Trudeau McBride believes that part of the "art spirit" is to give back to the community and nurture emerging artists. For thirty years, she has taught art to all age groups in private classes and by special invitation in the public education system. She operated her own art and gift gallery for several years.

An accomplished artist and painter, Wakie has studied with Jim Fallier, AWS; Milford Zornes, Sheila Parsons, Larry Weston, Tony Couch, Lola Doom, and others. Having produced and sold over 250 paintings, she has had many one-woman shows and won numerous awards. She and her artwork were featured in *Oklahoma Artists of Distinction*. Galleries across the United States have embraced and sold her art. She has also exhibited at the Arkansas Wildlife Federation show.

She has been a member of several art associations, including the Sequoyah County Arts and Humanities Council (serving four different terms as its president), the Crawford County Art Association, the Goddard Art Center, and the Ardmore Art Guild. She also helped organize the Arts and Humanities Council in Sallisaw, Oklahoma. Speaking on television or in person to numerous civic organizations, Wakie is an advocate for art as a way to create a balanced life.

In 2000, Wakie experienced a debilitating stroke one month after the loss of her husband. Finding herself unable to draw or paint, she did not give up. With prayer, occupational therapy, physical therapy, speech therapy, and a lot of determination, she began painting again. She started in oils because she had more time to think with oil than with watercolor, and the medium is more forgiving. Two and a half years later, she emerged more proficient than before the stroke.

Wakie wrote and illustrated *Drawing for All Ages* to continue sharing her love for art with more people. Her clear illustrations, beautiful paintings, and helpful instructions make drawing fun and easy for anyone wanting to learn to draw.

Sign up for the
TABLELAND PRESS newsletter

and receive the latest news on upcoming books,
plus devotionals, Christian book reviews, and Bible quizzes.

**Go to www.tablelandpress.com
today to sign up.**

As a Thank You, you will receive this FREE ebook!

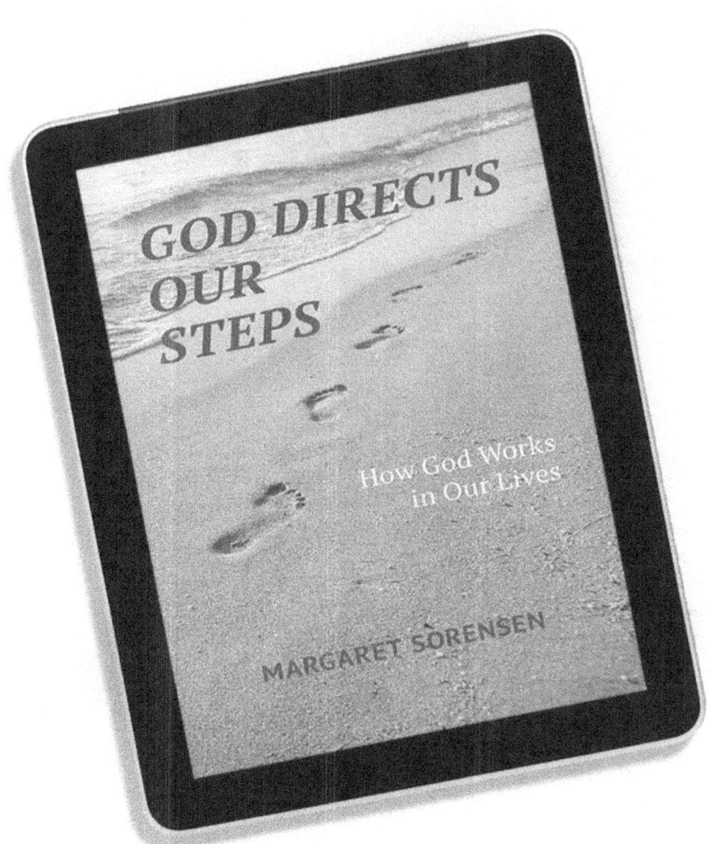

God Directs Our Steps
by Margaret Sorensen

Discover how God works
in your life by exploring
how He directed the paths
of eight biblical people.

Download your free PDF of *God Directs Our Steps*
at www.tablelandpress.com